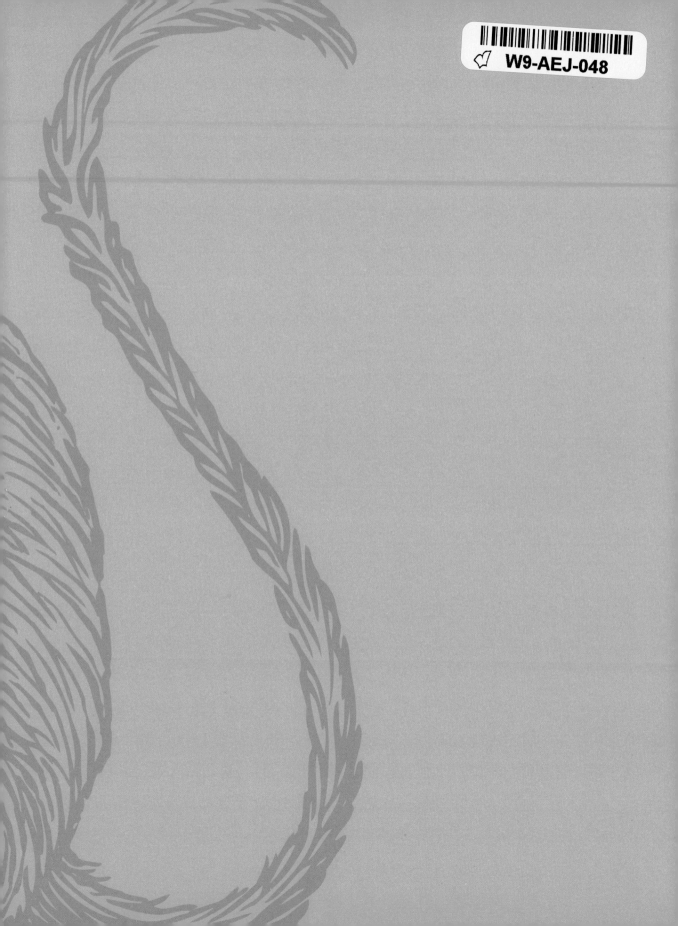

30 MINUTE
MOWGLI

30 MINUTE
MOWGLI

Fast Easy Indian from the Mowgli Home Kitchen

NISHA KATONA

NOURISH

EAT WELL, LIVE WELL

For my Mini and Beany, who have always "Stood at the crossroads and looked; asked for the ancient paths; asked where the good way was and walked in it".

30 Minute Mowgli
Nisha Katona

First published in the UK and USA in 2021 by
Nourish, an imprint of Watkins Media Limited
Unit 11, Shepperton House, 83–93 Shepperton Road
London N1 3DF

enquiries@nourishbooks.com

Publisher: Fiona Robertson
Project Editor: Daniel Hurst
Editorial assistant: Brittany Willis
Head of Design: Glen Wilkins
Production: Uzma Taj
Commissioned photography: Yuki Sugiura
(food) and Peter Goodbody (portraits)
Food Stylist: Claire Bassano
Art Director and Prop Stylist: Rachel Vere

A CIP record for this book is available from the
British Library

ISBN: 978-1-84899-400-3 (Hardback)
ISBN: 978-1-84899-404-1 (eBook)

10 9 8 7 6 5 4 3 2 1

Typeset in Futura and Minion Pro
Colour reproduction by XY Digital
Printed in China

Publisher's note
While every care has been taken in compiling the
recipes for this book, Watkins Media Limited, or any
other persons who have been involved in working on
this publication, cannot accept responsibility for any
errors or omissions, inadvertent or not, that may be
found in the recipes or text, nor for any problems that
may arise as a result of preparing one of these recipes.
If you are pregnant or breastfeeding or have any
special dietary requirements or medical conditions,
it is advisable to consult a medical professional before
following any of the recipes contained in this book.

Notes on the recipes
Unless otherwise stated:
Use medium fruit and vegetables
Use medium (US large) organic or free-range eggs
Use fresh herbs, spices and chillies
Use granulated sugar (Americans can use ordinary
granulated sugar when caster sugar is specified)
Do not mix metric, imperial and US cup measurements:
1 tsp = 5ml 1 tbsp = 15ml 1 cup = 240ml

nourishbooks.com

Contents

WELCOME   06

INTRODUCTION   10

POULTRY   30

MEAT   62

FISH   92

VEGETABLES AND PULSES   112

MA, LOOK AWAY!   156

DESSERTS AND DRINKS   170

INDEX   194

ACKNOWLEDGEMENTS   200

Welcome

When you pare back all the trappings of a busy life, it's good to be left with one passion that will see you through your twilight days. For me, that passion is cooking. And I don't mean elaborate or complicated cooking. In my two careers, firstly as a full-time barrister for over twenty years and then as an entrepreneur and restauranteur, there has never been much time at the end of the day to spend hours cooking up elaborate feasts in the kitchen. I get home, tired from the day's exertions, kick of my shoes and am faced with a household of hungry, expectant faces.

At these times, the act of pulling ingredients together into a meal that my family can sit and share together, comparing our battle scars from the day, is a reset between work and home life and an opportunity for some much-needed solitude and reflection as I stir a pot or gaze into the oven. These meals need to be quick and easy, otherwise the calming, restorative effects of cooking can quickly slip into resentment. On days like these, I am willing to wait 30 minutes for the alchemy of cooking to transform my hodgepodge of ingredients into something comforting and delicious, but no longer. And it is this way of cooking that forms the basis of this book.

My home kitchen is the genesis of all food that is served at the Mowgli restaurants, and though you will not find the long-simmered curries or slow-roasted meats that adorn Mowgli's menu within these pages, these recipes are what I actually cook at home on a daily basis; a distillation of the food that is served every day at Mowgli. Regardless of whether you are a guest in my home or are visiting one of my restaurants, the tenets of my food philosophy remain the same, and bold, vibrant flavour is at the heart of my cooking.

This is the type of cooking that I learnt growing up, both at home in Skelmersdale and on family trips back to visit our family in India, where, because of a lack of refrigeration combined with searing temperatures, ingredients had short shelf lives and, as such, would travel from market, to home, to pot in a matter of hours. Meals were planned, food was bought, food was cooked. There was no option or opportunity for waste.

Though times have changed and I could never live without the cool, sustaining power of my refrigerator now, I have the same attitude to waste and have tried to instil it in my own children. As such, this is not just a book about speed and simplicity. It's also about how to avoid waste and improvise with the things that lurk at the back and the bottom of your fridge. I have a particular passion for conjuring up a table full of food from all that is geriatric, shrivelled, dried and dormant in the kitchen. Where others may gaze forlornly at the past-their-best carrots or a few stalks of limp celery and lament that there is nothing to eat, I see only potential. A lack of choice is often the mother of invention, and pairing those sad-looking ingredients with spice, heat and perhaps a supplementary can or two from the back of your cupboard will transform them into something truly delicious. I come from a line of culinary wombles. We pride ourselves on using the things that people leave behind.

30 Minute Mowgli is the way that I cook every day. But rather beautifully, it's also the way that my ancestors – my grandmother and great-grandmother – cooked, with their small coal-fired stoves on their dusky Varanasi verandas. I hope, with this book, to bring you those big, instant flavours forged in the crucible of all that was humble and simple in the kitchens of my childhood.

Nisha Katona

8

INTRODUCTION

About This Book

When planning this book, I knew that I wanted these recipes to be true 30-minute wonders that could be on the table within half an hour of first reaching for a chopping board or putting a pan on the stove. I also knew that I wasn't willing to sacrifice on flavour in my quest for speed, and so quickly adopted the mantra of "big, instant flavour" when planning the recipes. If anything didn't succeed on both the time and flavour promises, then it didn't make it into the book. The third thing I knew was that I was opening myself up to criticism if people couldn't achieve the recipes within the 30-minute time frame. This is something that I have less control over, but all of the recipes have been tested my both myself and others, and I am very confident that they can be done. If anything does push the time frame for you the first time, then give it another go, and I hope you'll find that speed and familiarity go hand in hand.

The main course recipes are sorted into chapters on Poultry (p.30–61), Meat (p.62–91), Fish (p.92–111) and Vegetables and Pulses (p.112–155), with an additional outlier chapter called Ma, Look Away! (p.156–169). Though Indian food is in my bones, I am a culinary adulterer and love the velvety comfort of Italian food and the fresh, sharp vibrancy of Korean food. As such, no home-cooking book from me would be complete without a handful of recipes from each. Ma, Look Away! is custodian of those recipes that are regular, much-loved additions to my family table, yet have no place next to the recipes that I learnt at my mother's knee.

Throughout the chapters you will also find a smattering of Hungarian recipes. These could have been collected together and put in the Ma, Look Away! chapter along with the other non-Indian fare, but these are too precious and personal to my family to be treated as such. Much as many of my recipes have been passed down through the generations of my family, these have come to me through my husband's. My mother-in-law cooked me the Paprika Chicken recipe (p.40) on my first trip to Budapest to meet my husband's family 25 years ago and it has been part of my culinary armoury ever since, and the Little Sparrow Pea Soup (p.52) and After-School Pepper Pot (p.84) are recipes that I know that my girls will eventually cook for their own children. I hope that you love them as much as we do.

Because this book hinges on the idea that you can have a full meal on the table within 30 minutes or less, there is no place for side dishes in these chapters, and everything in the savoury sections is designed to happily feed four people in its own right, perhaps

with a little rice or some flatbreads on the side. The Vegetables and Pulses chapter contains more recipes than others in the book, partly because these ingredients in their many forms will live happily in the fridge, freezer and cupboard until they are called on, but also because I wanted this book to reflect the way the world eats. More and more people are cutting down on, or completely cutting out, meat and dairy every year and I wanted this book to cater for everyone. With that in mind, it's worth knowing that many of the poultry or meat recipes in the book can easily be adapted for vegetarians or vegans by substituting the meat for a similar weight of drained, canned butter/lima beans, or any other beans that you have in the cupboard, all of which soak up flavour wonderfully.

The Desserts and Drinks chapter (p.170–193) is slightly different in that, though the recipes conform to the 30-minute timescale, they are less used every day, or at least they are in my household, where we worship daily at the temple of savoury and only make the occasional pilgrimage to the gods of sweet. On those occasions when my sweet tooth calls, the need is often immediate, and these recipes will quickly satisfy those cravings. They also make wonderful options for nights when you are entertaining, as you can present something impressive to your guests with minimal time away from the table. This chapter is also home to the holy trinity of Indian drinks: a Mango and Mint Lassi (p.186), a traditional Masala Chai (p.188) and a Calcutta Cold Coffee (p.191). All of which will quench your thirst and awaken your tastebuds.

Big Instant Flavour

Spices are the building blocks of any curry. Each one has is its own distinct flavour and perfume and, added at the right time and in different combinations, they will transform your dishes from one-note to complex and flavourful. Having a well-stocked selection of spices is like having a flavour bank in your kitchen, where you can easily make withdrawals of fire, earth, sweet and sour at a moment's notice, so it is worth keeping track of those that you have and restocking any that are running low or are past their best.

Asian grocers or larger supermarkets with world-food aisles will often sell different spices in large bags, which can be much more economical than buying the smaller glass jars. That said, all spices have a shelf life and, unless you're going to using them regularly, it can be a false economy to buy them in such large amounts. Ground spices start to lose their potency around a year after being opened, so only buy the large bags if you will get through them in that time. Whole spices, such as cardamom pods or star anise, will keep happily in sealed jars for around two years.

While there are an intimidating array of spices available, I have tried to streamline those that are used in my recipes, much like choosing guests for a dinner party, only including those that bring real presence and personality. Those who bring "big, instant flavour". These are listed below and overleaf.

Ground Turmeric

The mother of all curry. To avoid burning, turmeric is added with other soft ingredients and provides an earthy foundation to curries. The flavour of sun-kissed Indian earth.

Chilli Powder

The father of all curry. Use in moderation to bring a gentle background of smoke. Add more if you want heat.

Garam Masala

The ultimate meat spice. All meat curries are based on this blend of up to 20 different spices. Buy a big bag and go in heavy.

Cumin Seeds

Cumin seeds govern many vegetarian Indian dishes. They need to be fried in oil to activate their full flavour.

Ground Coriander

Coriander provides a herby feminine note to curries that is subtle yet essential.

Ground Cumin

If you ever taste a curry and feel it's not "curry" enough, cumin powder adds that much-needed extra oomph.

Mustard Seeds

These must be fried in hot oil until they start to pop and taste like popcorn. They are divine cooked with leafy vegetables.

Nigella Seeds

These are the fish spice. They always go hand in hand with green chillies, dropped into hot oil at the start of most fish dishes.

Panch Phoron

This is the Bengali five-spice blend and is enigmatic and haunting. Fry this at the start of making your curry and produce that instant addictive flair.

Know Your Onions

While the key to the recipes in this book is speed, there is one ingredient that can't be rushed: onions. When cooked until soft and golden, onions lose their sharp pungency and take on a mellow sweetness as their natural sugars caramelize in the pan. When building a dish like a curry, this base note of sweetness is one of the key building blocks and simply cannot be rushed.

When instructing people on how to cook onions, I always say that the colour to aim for is "hotdog brown" – as close as possible to the gold, silky tangle that sits astride the best kind of hotdog. The onions in the bottom bowl in the picture opposite are there to act as a visual guide of what you are aiming for. Cooked in oil, it takes around 8 minutes to get onions to this stage. Turn the heat up too high and cook them too fast and your onions will burn and become acrid, so take the time to cook them properly and know that it will be worth the effort.

When it comes to chopping onions, I am more happy to cut corners. Most of the recipes in this book call for onions to be roughly chopped; there is neither time nor need for dicing finely here. Simply peel, top and tail your onions, cut them in half and pass your blade through them a few times on both axis to make neat chunks. When cooked as described above, these onions will break down and meld with your sauce, adding only a hint of extra bite. In sauces that are blended, you won't notice them at all.

Where recipes call for sliced onions, they don't need to be cut really finely, unless you are using them as a garnish (such as in my Ten-Minute, Late-Night Kebabs on p.86), as they will become soft and supple during cooking. The best and quickest way to slice an onion is to chop it in half through the root, then peel off the papery outer skin and slice off the pointy top. It is tempting to slice off the root, too, but keeping it intact will hold the onion together whilst you are slicing it and help keep the slices neat and uniform.

I haven't included recipes for pickles or chutneys in this book because of the 30-minute time limit and the knowledge that there are many wonderful varieties available in the shops, but the one exception to this is the recipe for Pink Pickled Onions that forms part of the Last-Minute Lamb Burgers (p.74). These only take moments to put together and keep wonderfully in the fridge for a few weeks, so I would urge you to keep a jar on hand. They add a glorious shock of pink to any plate and taste wonderful in toasted sandwiches, used to top a burger or to cut through the richness of a curry with their sharp astringency.

Shameless Shortcuts

In the quest to get a meal on the table in 30 minutes flat, I am happy to make only those concessions that will not impact negatively on the end result, but when I find brilliant shortcuts that truly make my life easier, I am evangelical about them. These are listed below.

Frozen Garlic and Ginger

When building a curry, especially a meat curry, the three base ingredients are always onions, garlic and ginger, in fairly large quantities – I always say, "as much as you can be bothered to chop!" As I've already mentioned, with onions there is no shortcut. However, garlic and ginger are a different story. While tubes of puréed garlic and ginger pastes are available, they can leave a vinegary, astringent taste and come in fairly small quantities. All is not lost though, and for the pure, unadulterated punch of flavour that these dishes need, frozen cubes of crushed garlic and ginger are an absolute wonder. Not only do they save masses of the time in the kitchen, but you can keep large bags of them in the freezer, so you always have a ready stock to hand. They are garlic and ginger, pure and simple, with the only added preservative coming courtesy of the deep freeze. Find them in the freezer section of Asian grocery stores or large supermarkets.
If I could only suggest one time-saving hack, it would be these.

The recipes in this book give quantities using both these cubes and also for fresh garlic and ginger, but as a rule of thumb, three cloves of garlic is equivalent to one garlic cube and a thumb-sized piece of ginger is the equivalent of one ginger cube.

To Peel or Not to Peel

I will rarely take the time to peel a potato. As long as they are scrubbed clean, then I will happily add them to whatever I am making. Keeping the skin on only adds to a dish, bringing the benefit of extra earthy flavour and fibre. There are exceptions to this rule, but added to a curry, stew or soup, there is no need to peel.

Preheating

This is obvious, but in terms of saving time in the kitchen, it is one of the biggest time savers. Before you reach for a chopping board or open the fridge to root for treasure inside, turn on your oven or grill/broiler to preheat. If you are deep frying, fill your

fryer or pan with oil and get it on the heat. If you don't, precious minutes will be lost while you wait for your cooking apparatus to come to temperature.

Frozen and Canned Spinach

In much the same way as garlic and ginger, you can't beat the convenience of frozen or canned spinach. The benefit here is perhaps less tangible, as wilting fresh spinach leaves is the work of moments, but when you take into account that one drained can or a few cubes of frozen spinach is the equivalent to that large bag of fresh spinach taking up space in your fridge, and that frozen or canned spinach will sit dormant in your cupboard or freezer for months on end, then the benefit becomes immediately obvious.

Poultry and Meat

When cooking chicken or meat, Indian cooks will almost always opt for bone-in. This is because, once cooked, bones release an incredible amount of flavour that you simply will not find in a chicken breast or lean cut of meat. The problem is that meat on the bone does take longer to cook, as the heat has to permeate right into those bones before they release their sacred juices. Because of the time restraints here, cooking meat on the bone is not an option, but there are a few tricks we can employ to get that extra oomph of meaty flavour into our dishes.

When cooking larger pieces of chicken either under the grill/broiler or on the barbecue, I have opted for boneless, skin-on chicken thighs. It's no secret that the darker meat of the thigh is more flavourful (and cheaper) than breast, and the fats held in the skin will release flavour and baste the meat in their juices as they cook, resulting in meat that is juicy and full of flavour.

When cooking meat, there are no long simmers in this book and, as such, we need access to immediate flavour. Look for well-marbled cuts where the fat will render down and baste the meat as it cooks. For curries, meatballs made from minced/ground meat are a wonderful way of making a tasty meat curry that is tender, full of flavour and can be cooked quickly. You will find a couple of examples in this book.

The 30-Minute Storecupboard

A well-stocked storecupboard is the ready barracks of any kitchen. These are humble ingredients that don't jostle for position in the fridge, desperate for a moment in the sun before their time runs out. These are the supporting cast and, as such, those that carry the whole production. I am talking everything from canned vegetables, pulses and legumes, to oils, spices and vinegars, and rice, grains and pastas, and that is only scratching the surface. With such a miscellany of contents, it's important to try and organise your cupboards in a way that makes sense to you and to keep track of which items are running low. This isn't about instagrammable glass jars or beautiful hand-written labels, though those have their place, it's about practicality and functionality. My storecupboards, and if you're going to be cooking regularly from this book, I would suggest yours also, will always be brimming with the following items.

Canned Goods

When the fridge is bare I always have an artillery of canned vegetables and legumes to fall back on. Canned chopped tomatoes form the basis of so many dishes, but I also couldn't get by without canned lentils, butter/lima beans, spinach, chickpeas/garbanzo beans and coconut milk.

Stock Cubes

Stock cubes, particularly ham stock cubes, are a great way of adding instant oomph to a dish. They add a salty, sweet hit that one usually only gets from the long simmer of bone in meat cuts. As a speedy substitute these are wonderful, so hold your head up high and invest in a little artillery of shameless cuboid assistants.

English Mustard

Added to the end of a curry, English mustard adds an extra zing that is hard to beat. It makes a wonderful addition to any tomato-based sauce. Despite its name, mustard seed has been prized in Indian cooking for thousands of years and the punch of ready-made mustard paste rounds off a curry wonderfully.

Oil

In most of my recipes I use vegetable oil. When cooking curries, frying the spices in oil awakens their flavour, which in turn flavours the oil they are cooked in, so it is best to start with as neutral a flavoured oil as possible.

Sugar

Indian cooks season their dishes with salt and sugar, and you will find that many of the dishes in this book gave a spoonful or two of brown sugar added near the end of cooking. Curries are a balance of spice, salt and sweet, so I encourage you to taste and season your recipes as you go.

Rice and Breads

When thinking of Indian food there is a tendency to picture a table groaning with a vast array of dishes. There is a nugget of truth in this, and when entertaining, the Indian cook can expect to be judged harshly if the selection offered to guests is too meagre, but that is not the type of cooking that is at the heart of this book. The recipes in these pages are all designed to happily feed four people in their own right, without the need for additional sides that would push the cooking time well beyond the 30-minute limit. That kind of culinary juggling act is best saved for when you have a houseful of guests and plenty of time to prepare, not on a Tuesday night when the kids are circling with a hungry look in their eyes and you've had a busy day at work.

This is also the reason why you won't find recipes for naan, rotis or puris here. Indian breads are readily available from supermarkets and can be reheated in moments, so save yourself the effort and add a couple to your weekly shop. I will often eat a curry simply with a roti (or even a tortilla wrap) alongside for scooping up the juices.

Black Cardamom Rice

This is my go-to recipe and can easily be made alongside any of the dishes in this book without hampering your cooking times. It is the same recipe included in *Mowgli Street Food*, for which I hope you'll forgive me, but it has been in my family for over a hundred years, so could not be replaced.

Serves 4
190g/6½oz/scant 1 cup basmati rice
3 black cardamom pods
1 tbsp vegetable oil
1 tsp cumin seeds

1 Rinse the rice under running water until it runs clear, then drain and put in a saucepan with the cardamom pods and 450ml/15fl oz/1¾ cups of water. Bring to the boil, then reduce to a simmer and cook for 10 minutes, uncovered, until almost dry with a dimpled surface. Cover the pan, remove from the heat and leave to stand for 10–15 minutes.

2 Meanwhile, heat the oil in a small frying pan/skillet and fry the cumin seeds till fragrant and dark golden brown. Fluff up the rice with a fork, then stir through the cumin seeds and serve.

1
POULTRY

I love cooking with poultry because it is so yielding and absorbent, quickly taking on the fragrance of the spices and herbs in which it is simmered or marinated. Chopped up small, it also works wonderfully for quick cooking, making the perfect base for speedy curries or stews.

Traditionally, Indian cooks would always use meat on the bone, but that requires a longer cook than we have time for here. For dishes that require larger pieces of chicken, I have opted for boneless, skin-on chicken thighs, which retain the finger-licking juiciness and depth of flavour that we are looking for, but can be cooked quickly.

This chapter is all about big, one-pot crowd-pleasers that can be on the table with minimal fuss. Something that chicken does so uniquely well.

There are speedy versions of some Mowgli classics, such as the Quick Angry Tandoori (p.46) which is a 30-minute version of the Angry Bird recipe from my first book. Because we are sacrificing the marinating time, it is important to slash the flesh so that the flavours of the marinade can quickly permeate into the chicken. That done, the result will be juicy and packed with more flavour than you would believe possible in the time given.

Chicken Dhansak

If you want hearty, you want Dhansak! Bulking out a pan of chicken curry with lentils is a wonderful way of stretching a dish when you have lots of mouths to feed. Red lentils work wonderfully here as they are quick to cook and make for a lovely thick sauce that allows the beautifully fragrant spices of the curry to shine through.

SERVES 4

120ml/4fl oz/½ cup vegetable oil

2 onions, roughly chopped

2 cubes frozen crushed garlic
    or 6 garlic cloves, crushed

2 cubes frozen crushed ginger
    or 2 thumb-sized pieces fresh
    ginger, peeled and grated

3 fat green chillies, left whole

3 tbsp garam masala

1 tbsp ground cumin

¼ tsp chilli powder

1 tsp ground turmeric

3 skinless, boneless chicken breasts
    (approx. 600g 1lb 5oz), chopped
    into 2cm/¾in cubes

400g/14oz canned chopped tomatoes

200g/7oz/generous 1 cup dried red
    lentils

1½ tsp salt

1 tsp sugar

juice of ½ lemon

100g/3½oz baby spinach leaves

small handful fresh coriander/cilantro,
    finely chopped

cooked rice or flatbreads, to serve

1 Heat the oil in a large, heavy-based pan over a medium-high heat. Add the onions, garlic, ginger and whole chillies and cook, stirring continuously, for 5 minutes, until the onions are soft and starting to turn golden brown.

2 Add the spices to the pan along with the chopped chicken breasts, stirring to coat the chicken and onions in the spices. Add the chopped tomatoes, lentils, salt, sugar and 800ml/27fl oz/3⅓ cups of boiling water to the pan and stir to combine. Bring to a boil, then reduce the heat to a lively simmer and leave to cook, uncovered, for 15 minutes, until the lentils are soft.

3 Add the lemon juice to the pan and taste the sauce, adding more salt and sugar if necessary, then stir the spinach leaves through the curry and leave to cook for 5 minutes more, until the spinach has wilted.

4 Stir the coriander/cilantro through the curry and remove the pan from the heat. Serve the Dhansak hot with your choice of cooked rice or flatbreads alongside.

Mango Chicken Curry

My mother has such disdain for fruit in curry. Mrs Beeton had other ideas with her chicken curries laced with spoonfuls of mango chutney – a real toe curler for any real Indian! Personally, I sit on the fence, and I love the sweetness and zing mango gives to this dish. I've opted for fresh mango, but frozen or tinned work just as well if the fruit is out of season or too expensive. Embrace the fruity subversion, but don't tell Ma!

SERVES 4

120ml/4 fl oz/½ cup vegetable oil
2 onions, roughly chopped.
2 cubes frozen crushed ginger
    or 2 thumb-sized pieces fresh
    root ginger, peeled and grated
2 cubes frozen crushed garlic
    or 6 garlic cloves, crushed
2 tbsp garam masala
1 tbsp ground coriander
1 tsp ground turmeric
2 fat green chillies, roughly chopped

3 skinless, boneless chicken breasts
    (approx. 600g/1lb 5oz),
    chopped into 2cm/¾in cubes
1 mango, peeled, stoned and
    chopped into 1cm/½in pieces
1½ tsp salt
2 tbsp sugar
2 tbsp ground almonds
200ml/7fl oz/1 cup crème fraîche
small handful fresh coriander/cilantro,
    finely chopped
cooked rice, or flatbreads, to serve

1 Heat the oil in a large pan over a medium heat, then add the onions and cook, stirring occasionally, for 6 minutes. Add the garlic and ginger and cook for another 2 minutes, until the onions are soft and golden brown. Add the garam masala, ground coriander, ground turmeric, chopped green chillies and chicken breasts, and cook, stirring, for 3 minutes to seal the chicken and coat it in the spices.

2 Add the chopped mango, salt and 400ml/14fl oz of boiling water to the pan and stir to combine. Bring to the boil, then reduce the heat to a simmer, cover with a lid and leave to cook for 12 minutes, until the chicken is cooked through and the sauce has thickened and reduced. Remove from the heat and stir through the sugar, almonds, crème fraîche and coriander/cilantro. Serve hot, with your choice of rice or flatbreads alongside.

Chicken, Coconut and Pineapple Curry

The combination of both coconut milk and creamed coconut in this curry adds a real gloss and weight to the sauce, giving it a gorgeous, velvety texture. If you can't get creamed coconut just double-up on the tinned. During the last moments of these exotic sunshine curries, I often throw a handful of roasted nuts to boost the salt and the beach-holiday feel. If you're not a fan of nuts or don't have any to hand, you can leave these out without any detriment to the dish.

SERVES 4

2 thumb-sized pieces fresh root
    ginger, peeled
5 tbsp vegetable oil
2 onions, finely chopped
2 cloves garlic, crushed
3 skinless, boneless chicken breasts
    (approx. 600g/1lb 5oz),
    chopped into 2cm/¾in cubes
2 tbsp garam masala
1 heaped tsp ground coriander
1 tsp ground turmeric
¼ tsp chilli powder

100g/3½oz creamed coconut
400ml/14fl oz canned coconut milk
2 green chillies, finely sliced
1½ tsp salt
1 tsp brown sugar
10 chunks canned pineapple, cut into
    1–2cm/½–¾in pieces
100g/3½oz roasted salted cashew nuts
small handful fresh coriander/cilantro,
    finely chopped, to garnish
1 red chilli, finely sliced, to garnish
cooked rice, or flatbreads, to serve

1 Finely mince one of the pieces of ginger and slice the other into fine matchsticks. Set aside.

2 Heat the oil in a large pan over a medium heat. Add the onions, garlic and minced ginger and fry, stirring continuously, for 8 minutes, until golden brown. Add the chicken to the pan and stir to combine with the onions, then add the garam masala, ground coriander, ground turmeric and chilli powder. Cook, stirring occasionally, for 5 minutes, to seal the chicken and coat it in the spices.

3 Add the creamed coconut, coconut milk, ginger matchsticks, sliced chillies, salt, sugar, pineapple and cashews to the pan and stir to combine, adding a little of the juice from the canned pineapple if the mixture is too dry. Leave to cook, stirring occasionally, for 5–10 minutes, until the chicken is cooked through. Scatter with chopped coriander/cilantro and sliced red chilli, then serve hot with rice or wraps alongside.

Paprika Chicken

This is my mother-in-law's recipe and was one of the dishes she cooked for me when I met her for the first time in Budapest. My husband is Hungarian and our first date, over 25 years ago, was at an Indian restaurant in Lamb's Conduit Street, London. It was a test of sorts, as I knew that if he didn't love my food, then the relationship wasn't going anywhere! I ordered him a chicken tikka masala, his first ever curry and one that often acts as a gateway into Indian cuisine. In much the same way, Paprika Chicken is at the heart of Hungarian cuisine, and both dishes beckon newcomers beautifully into the heart of our culinary cultures with their deep red promise and big arresting flavours.

SERVES 4

100ml/3½fl oz/scant ½ cup
   vegetable oil
2 onions, roughly chopped
2 cubes frozen crushed garlic
   or 6 garlic cloves, crushed
2 tbsp paprika
3 skinless, boneless chicken breasts
   (approx. 600g/1lb 5oz),
   chopped into 2cm/¾in cubes

1 chicken stock cube, crumbled
200g/7oz canned chopped tomatoes
1 tsp sugar
1 tsp salt
4 tbsp sour cream
small handful fresh parsley, leaves
   picked and chopped
cooked rice, to serve

1 Heat the oil in a large pan over a medium heat, then add the onions and cook, stirring occasionally, for 6 minutes. Add the garlic and cook for 2 minutes, until the onions are golden brown. Add the paprika and cook, stirring to coat the onions, for another 2 minutes.

2 Add the chicken to the pan and stir to coat in the onion and spices. Cook for 2 minutes, stirring continuously, to seal the chicken, then crumble in the stock cube and add the chopped tomatoes, sugar, salt and 200ml/7fl oz of boiling water. Give everything a good stir to combine, then bring to the boil, reduce the heat to a simmer and leave to cook 15 minutes, stirring occasionally, until the chicken is cooked through. Remove the pan from the heat and stir through the sour cream and parsley. Serve hot with cooked rice alongside.

40

Chicken and Spinach Curry

On approaching every family meal, I think about how, in one pan, I can incorporate as many of our five-a-day as possible. Adding in spinach is a brilliant way to shovel loads of goodness into children without them batting an eye. When my kids were growing up they dubbed this "Gollum Chicken Curry" because of its sludgy appearance. In contrast, I had hoped to be able to call it "Emerald Chicken Curry" but that is not how spinach behaves. It concentrates only on giving body and beautiful flavour, which suits me down to the ground.

SERVES 4

120ml/4fl oz/½ cup vegetable oil

2 onions, roughly chopped

2 cubes frozen crushed garlic
    or 6 garlic cloves, crushed

2 cubes frozen crushed ginger
    or 2 thumb-sized pieces fresh
    root ginger, peeled and grated

5 dried curry leaves

1 tsp ground turmeric

¼ tsp chilli powder

1 tbsp ground cumin

2 tbsp ground coriander

200g/7oz canned chopped tomatoes

1 tbsp tomato purée

400g/14oz canned leaf spinach or
    5 cubes frozen spinach (defrosted)
    or 1 small bag of fresh spinach

15g coriander/cilantro, roughly
    chopped, plus extra for serving

1½ tsp salt, or to taste

3 skinless, boneless chicken breasts
    (approx. 600g/1lb 5oz), chopped
    into 2cm/¾in cubes

cooked rice, to serve

1 Heat the oil in a large pan over a medium heat. Add the onions and cook, stirring continuously, for 6 minutes, until soft and translucent, then add the garlic, ginger and curry leaves and cook for a further 2 minutes, until the onions have started to turn golden brown. Add the spices to the pan and stir to coat the onions, then stir in the chopped tomatoes and tomato purée. Drain the canned spinach and stir through the mixture, then pour in 300ml/10fl oz/½ pint of boiling water and stir again to loosen. Add the chopped coriander/cilantro to the sauce and season with the salt to taste. Remove the pan from the heat, then use a stick/immersion blender to purée the sauce until smooth.

2 Return the pan to the heat and add the chopped chicken breasts, stirring to coat the chicken in the sauce. Bring the sauce to a gentle simmer, then reduce the heat to low, cover the pan with a lid and leave to cook for 12–15 minutes, until the chicken is cooked through. Serve the curry hot with rice alongside and a scattering of fresh coriander/cilantro.

Chicken Korma

Often seen as a gateway curry, due to its creamy sauce and polite spicing, a well-made korma can be a wonderful thing. Unlike the kormas that many will be familiar with, this uses crème fraîche as a base, rather than cream, for a lighter, tangier result.

SERVES 4

120ml/4fl oz/½ cup vegetable oil
2 onions, roughly chopped
2 cubes frozen crushed garlic
    or 6 garlic cloves, crushed
2 cubes frozen crushed ginger
    or 2 thumb-sized pieces fresh
    ginger, peeled and grated
2 tbsp garam masala
¼ tsp chilli powder
1 tsp ground turmeric

3 skinless, boneless chicken breasts
    (approx. 600g/1lb 5oz),
    chopped into 2cm/¾in cubes
1½ tsp salt
2½ tbsp sugar
2 tbsp ground almonds
200ml/7fl oz/scant 1 cup crème fraîche
cooked rice, to serve
small bunch of coriander/cilantro,
    roughly chopped, to garnish

1 Heat the oil in a large frying pan/skillet over a medium heat. Add the onions and cook, stirring continuously, for 6 minutes, until soft and translucent, then add the garlic and ginger and cook for a further 2 minutes, until the onions have started to turn golden brown.

2 Add the garam masala, chilli powder, ground turmeric and chopped chicken breasts and cook, stirring continuously, for 3 minutes until the chicken is starting to brown and is well coated in the spices.

3 Add 400ml/14 fl oz/1⅔ cups of boiling water to the pan along with the salt and stir to combine. Bring the mixture to the boil, then reduce the heat to a lively simmer and leave to cook, uncovered, for 12 minutes or until the chicken is cooked through and the sauce is substantially reduced.

4 Remove the pan from the heat and stir the sugar, almonds and crème fraîche through the mixture. Serve the korma hot with rice alongside and garnished with fresh coriander/cilantro.

Quick Angry Tandoori

This is such a great dish to cook in the oven or on a barbecue. The marinade is textbook tandoori and the acids from the lemon and yoghurt mean that it is ready to go within minutes of being prepped, or is even better if you prep it and leave it covered in the fridge for a day or two before cooking. Slashing the flesh helps with making sure the flavours find their way into the flesh, but this really is a rub and go.

SERVES 4

100ml/3½fl oz/scant ½ cup
   vegetable oil
300g/10½oz/scant 3 cups plain
   yoghurt
3 cloves garlic, crushed
2 cubes frozen crushed ginger,
   defrosted or 2 thumb-sized pieces
   fresh ginger, peeled and grated

1 tsp ground turmeric
1 tsp chilli powder
1 tbsp ground cumin
2 tbsp garam masala
3 tbsp sweet paprika
2 tsp salt
juice of ½ lemon
1kg/2lb 4oz skin-on, boneless
   chicken thighs, lightly slashed

1 Preheat the oven to 220°C/425°F/gas mark 7 and line a baking sheet with foil.

2 Put all the ingredients except the chicken in a large bowl and stir to combine. Add the chicken to the bowl and use your hands to massage the marinade into the chicken flesh, ensuring it is really well coated. Transfer the chicken to the baking sheet in a single layer and bake in the oven for 20–25 minutes, until the chicken is tender, golden and beginning to char slightly at the edges. Serve hot.

Chicken Kofta Curry

I love turning a bowl of minced/ground meat into flavoured meatballs or "koftas", as you can really tailor them to what you fancy (and have to hand). I always add a few spices, but you can also add fresh or dried herbs to the mix for a different bomb of flavour every time.

SERVES 4

100ml/3½fl oz/½ cup vegetable oil
1½ tsp black mustard seeds
2 onions, roughly chopped
2 cubes frozen crushed garlic
    or 6 garlic cloves, crushed
2 cubes frozen crushed ginger
    or 2 thumb-sized pieces fresh
    ginger, peeled and grated
5 dried curry leaves
2 fat green chillies, roughly chopped
100g/3½oz creamed coconut, grated
200ml/7fl oz/scant 1 cup coconut milk
1 tsp ground turmeric
¼ tsp chilli powder

2 tbsp garam masala
1½ tbsp ground coriander
1 tsp sugar
2 tsp salt
200ml/7fl oz/scant 1 cup crème fraîche
small handful coriander/cilantro, roughly
    chopped, to garnish
cooked rice or flatbreads, to serve

For the koftas:
500g/1lb 2oz minced/ground chicken
2 tbsp ground coriander
1 tsp salt
30g/1oz fresh chives, finely chopped

1 Heat the oil in a large pan over a medium heat. Add the mustard seeds and fry until they start to crackle and pop, then add the onions and cook, stirring continuously, for 6 minutes, until soft and translucent. Add the garlic, ginger, curry leaves and chopped chillies to the pan and cook, stirring, for another 2 minutes, until the onions have started to turn golden brown.

2 Meanwhile, put all the ingredients for the koftas in a large bowl and mix until really well combined. Take handfuls of the mixture and roll into golf ball-sized balls with your hands, then set them aside while you repeat the process until all of the mixture is used up.

3 Once the onions are cooked, reduce the heat to low and stir in the creamed coconut, coconut milk and 800ml/27fl oz/3⅓ cups of boiling water. Add the ground turmeric, chilli powder, garam masala, ground coriander, sugar and salt to the pan and stir again to combine.

4 Once the mixture is bubbling, drop the kofta into the curry and stir to coat in the sauce. Cover the pan with a lid and leave for 5–6 minutes, until the koftas are cooked through.

5 Remove the lid from the pan and stir the crème fraîche through the curry. Garnish the dish with a handful of fresh coriander/cilantro and serve hot with rice or flatbreads alongside.

Sticky Chicken Thighs

In a cheffy way of which I'm not proud, I have previously always hated the idea of cooking with ketchup, but despite my snooty tendencies, I now have to admit that nothing else works quite like it for adding an instant sweet and sticky balance to these barbecue-style marinades. I now find myself so brazenly ensconced in the cult of ketchup that here I have embraced its swaggering joy in one of my sticky family heirloom recipes.

SERVES 4
2 heaped tbsp tomato purée
juice of ½ lemon
2 cloves garlic, crushed
2 tbsp garam masala
1 tbsp paprika

1 tsp fenugreek powder
125ml/4fl oz/½ cup tomato ketchup
4 tbsp runny honey
8 skin-on, boneless chicken thighs
salad, to serve

1 Preheat the grill/broiler to high and line a grill pan with foil, or prepare a barbecue/grill for cooking.

2 Put all the ingredients except the chicken in a large bowl and stir to combine. Add the chicken to the bowl and use your hands to massage the marinade into the chicken flesh, ensuring it is really well coated.

3 Cook the chicken under the grill or on the barbecue for 6–8 minutes on each side, or until the chicken is tender, golden and beginning to char slightly at the edges. Serve hot with your choice of salad alongside.

51

Little Sparrow Pea Soup

In Eastern Europe these clear soups are a very big deal. And it's no wonder – they are filling, warming and utterly satisfying. The playful little gnarled dumplings are a real winner with children – in Hungary they are called *Knockerdli*, and in Germany they are *Spaetzle* or "little sparrows". I make them by running a thick batter through a colander into the boiling soup, which adds a fun element of theatre to the homeliest of dishes.

SERVES 4
2 tbsp vegetable oil
50g/1¾oz chorizo, finely diced
2 cubes frozen crushed garlic
    or 6 garlic cloves, crushed
2 large tomatoes, roughly chopped
2 carrots, peeled and finely sliced
1 parsnip, peeled and finely sliced
1 tbsp paprika
3 chicken stock cubes, crumbled

2 tsp salt
1 tsp sugar
100g/3½oz/⅔ cup frozen peas
small handful parsley, leaves picked
    and chopped

For the dumplings:
125g/4½oz plain flour
pinch of salt
1 egg

1 To make the soup, heat the oil in a large pan over a medium heat. Add the chorizo and cook, stirring for 2 minutes, until the chorizo is golden and has released its oil. Reduce the heat to low, then add the garlic and cook, stirring continuously, for another 2 minutes, being careful not to burn it. Add the tomatoes, carrots, parsnips and paprika to the pan and stir to coat for 1 minute, then pour in 1.4l/2½ pints/scant 6 cups of boiling water and crumble in the stock cubes. Bring the mixture to the boil, season to taste with the salt and sugar, then reduce to a simmer and leave to cook for 5–10 minutes, until the carrots and parsnips are tender.

2 Meanwhile, prepare the dumplings. Sift the flour into a large bowl and add the salt. Make a well in the flour and crack in the egg, then stir to combine with the flour. Gradually pour in enough cold water to make a thick, pourable batter, whisking the mixture until smooth.

3 Add the peas to the soup and cook for 2–3 minutes, until tender. Hold a large-holed colander over the pan of soup and pour the dumpling batter through it, using a wooden spoon to press it down as necessary. As the drops of batter hit the hot soup, they will form tiny dumplings. Once all of the batter has passed through the colander, give the soup a stir and leave to cook 3–4 minutes. Stir through the chopped parsley, ladle into serving bowls and serve hot.

Yoghurt and Coriander Turkey with Tenderstem Broccoli

Turkey is often regarded as a dry and unyielding meat. We all know it is very lean and very healthy and that it *can* be very delicious, but how to achieve that? I find this way of cooking turkey breast steaks to be absolutely marvellous at producing juicy, tender results. Yoghurt is a great tenderiser and melds with the turkey to make it juicy and flavourful. This is wonderful made on the hoof, as described here, but if you have the foresight to marinate these the day before, by the time you come to cook the turkey, it will have almost cooked itself in the tangy marinade.

SERVES 4

300ml/10fl oz/1¼ cups plain yoghurt
1½ tsp salt
2 tbsp garlic purée
2 tbsp ground coriander
3 tbsp olive oil

freshly ground black pepper
4 turkey steaks (approx. 450g/1lb)
juice of ½ lemon
200g/7oz tenderstem broccoli
1 tsp mustard seeds
½ clove garlic, crushed

1 Preheat the grill/broiler to high and line a grill pan with foil.

2 Put the plain yoghurt, salt, garlic purée, ground coriander, 1 tablespoon of the oil and a generous grinding of pepper in a large bowl and stir to combine. Add the turkey steaks to the bowl and use your hands to massage the marinade into the turkey flesh. Add the lemon juice to the bowl and massage again, ensuring the turkey is really well coated.

3 Lay the turkey flat on the grill pan and place under the grill to cook for 5–6 minutes on each side, until the turkey is cooked through.

4 Meanwhile, put the broccoli in a steamer and cook for 5–6 minutes, until tender.

5 Heat the remaining oil in a small frying pan/skillet over a medium heat. Add the mustard seeds and cook until they start to pop and turn grey. Add the garlic to the pan and stir for 30 seconds, being careful not to burn, then remove the pan from the heat and toss the broccoli in the flavoured oil.

6 Divide the cooked turkey steaks between serving plates and serve with the tenderstem broccoli alongside.

54

Mowgli Coleslaw Chicken Bowl

Coleslaw is something of an obsession of mine, and I'm always inventing new and exciting twists to add extra texture or make the dressing really sing. This slaw is completely delicious on its own, but paired with succulent, crisp and spicy chicken, it makes for a wonderfully light, fresh and warming supper.

SERVES 4

For the Coleslaw:
½ small white cabbage, shredded
2 large carrots, peeled and grated
1 red onion, halved and finely sliced
1 apple, peeled, cored and grated
100g/3½oz mayonnaise
1 tsp salt
juice of ½ lemon
1 tbsp vegetable oil
1 tbsp mustard seed

For the Crispy Paprika Chicken:
3 tbsp plain flour
1 tsp paprika
½ tsp salt
½ tsp ground black pepper
400g/14oz chicken mini fillets
1 egg
100g/3½oz/2 cups white breadcrumbs
vegetable oil, for shallow frying

1 First, prepare the coleslaw. Using a food processor fitted with a blade, prepare all your vegetables. (You can also do this by hand, but it will take longer.) Put all of the prepared vegetables in a large bowl and add the mayonnaise, salt and lemon juice. Stir to combine.

2 Heat the oil in a frying pan/skillet over a medium heat, then add the mustard seeds and cook until they start to pop and turn grey. Pour the oil and mustard seeds onto the coleslaw, then toss everything together and set aside while you prepare the chicken.

3 Set 3 wide, shallow bowls next to each other on the worktop. Put the flour, paprika, salt and black pepper in the first bowl and stir to combine. Crack and beat the egg into the second bowl and put the breadcrumbs in the third bowl.

4 Working with one mini fillet at a time, toss the chicken in the seasoned flour, then dip into the egg, then roll in the breadcrumbs to coat. Set aside while you repeat the process with the remaining pieces of chicken.

5 Put a large frying pan over a medium heat and add vegetable oil to a depth of 2cm/¾in. Once the oil is hot, add the chicken to the pan in batches and fry for 2 minutes on each side, until golden and cooked through.

6 Divide the coleslaw into serving bowls and top each with a few pieces of crispy chicken, or just put everything in the middle of the table and let everyone dig in themselves.

Monsoon Chicken and Mushroom Curry

In her youth, my mother would only be able to get mushrooms in India during the monsoon season when corners of her village became dark and dank. Mushrooms struggled in the stark sunlight and the heat of the rest of the year. This was a special time for my mother because mushroom curry finally made the menu. Being bound to such seasonal ingredients really makes one appreciate what to us in the west seems so mundane and every day. Hopefully you will appreciate them as my mother did in this fantastic curry, where they simmer, soften and transform in the warming curry spices.

SERVES 4

120ml/4fl oz/½ cup vegetable oil
2 onions, roughly chopped
2 cubes frozen crushed garlic
    or 6 garlic cloves, crushed
2 cubes frozen crushed ginger
    or 2 thumb-sized pieces fresh
    root ginger, peeled and grated
3 fat green chillies
3 skinless, boneless chicken breasts
    (approx. 600g/1lb 5oz),
    chopped into 2cm/¾in cubes

3 tbsp garam masala
1 tbsp ground cumin
¼ tsp chilli powder
1 tsp ground turmeric
400g/14oz canned chopped tomatoes
1 tsp salt
1 tsp sugar
250g/9oz chestnut/cremini mushrooms,
    thickly sliced
small handful fresh coriander/cilantro,
    finely chopped, to garnish
cooked rice or flatbreads, to serve

1 Heat the oil in a large pan over a medium heat. Add the onions, garlic, ginger and whole green chillies and fry, stirring continuously, for 8 minutes, until golden brown. Add the chicken to the pan and stir to combine with the onions, then add the garam masala, ground cumin, chilli powder and ground turmeric. Cook, stirring occasionally, for 3 minutes, to seal the chicken and coat it in the spices.

2 Add the chopped tomatoes, salt, sugar and 400ml/14fl oz of boiling water and stir to combine. Bring to the boil, then reduce the heat to a simmer and cook, stirring occasionally, for 5 minutes. Add the mushrooms to the pan and stir to combine, then leave to cook, stirring occasionally, for another 10 minutes, until the chicken is cooked through and the mushrooms are tender. Serve the curry hot, scattered with fresh coriander/cilantro and with your choice of cooked rice or flatbreads alongside.

Chicken Papaya
and Green Bean Keema

In India, green papaya is very commonly used to tenderise meat. The acids in the fruit help to soften the meat and encourage it to absorb flavours and spices. I love adding papaya to minced/ground meat that is cooked with simple curry spices, as it imparts a lovely freshness of flavour. The addition of green beans (or any vegetable that you have to use up lurking at the back of your fridge), has the double benefit of making this delicious keema go a bit further, and also makes it so very good for you.

SERVES 4

2 tbsp vegetable oil
2 onions, roughly chopped
2 cubes frozen crushed ginger
 or 2 thumb-sized pieces fresh
 ginger, peeled and grated
2 cubes frozen crushed garlic
 or 6 garlic cloves, crushed
100g/3½oz fine green beans,
 cut into thirds
1 green chilli, sliced
400g/14oz minced/ground chicken

1 tsp ground turmeric
¼ tsp chilli powder
1 tbsp garam masala
2 tsp ground cumin
400g/14oz canned chopped tomatoes
2 papayas, peeled, deseeded and
 roughly chopped
1½ tsp salt, or to taste
1 tsp sugar
squeeze of lemon juice
small handful fresh coriander/cilantro,
 chopped, to garnish

1 Heat the oil in a large frying pan/skillet over a medium heat. Add the onions, ginger and garlic and cook, stirring continuously, for 8 minutes, until the onions are golden brown.

2 Add the green beans, sliced chilli and minced/ground chicken and cook, stirring continuously, for 3 minutes, until the chicken has browned. Add the spices to the pan and cook, stirring continuously, for a further 2 minutes.

3 Add the chopped tomatoes to the pan along with 400ml/14fl oz/generous 1½ cups of water and stir the mixture to combine. Once the contents of the pan is bubbling, reduce the heat to a simmer and leave to cook for 5–8 minutes. You can tell the curry is ready when the oil rises to the surface and forms a golden ring around the edge of the pan.

4 Add the chopped papayas to the pan, stir, then season to taste with the salt, sugar and a squeeze of lemon juice. Finally, stir through the chopped coriander/cilantro, spoon the keema into serving bowls and serve hot.

2
MEAT

The secret to cooking red meat quickly is to choose steaks that are richly marbled with fat. As the meat cooks it renders down for a quick and moist finish, with a great degree of self basting. Another benefit of marbled meat is that it also absorbs flavours more quickly than leaner cuts.

Any of the grilled/broiled meat recipes in this chapter would be a wonderful addition to a barbecue; just make sure your coals are roasting hot before you start to cook and the cooking times should be more or less the same.

The fastest way to cook beef, lamb or pork will come from any kind of minced/ground meat. My Spinach Meatball Curry (p.80) or Minced Pork and Glass Noodle Broth (p.90) are both super quick and full of deep, impactful flavour.

The flavour combinations and marinades here would also work brilliantly with poultry, or even fish, so feel free to pick and choose elements and reinvent them into entirely new dishes as you see fit.

Gingerbread Lamb Steaks

I invented this dish a few years ago when I was on the way to the bin to dispose of an old gingerbread house that my daughter had made. It was in late January and I was preparing a dramatic lamb *raan*, with a hearty punch of warming spice. In a moment of inspiration, I tipped the gingerbread house, icing and all, into the marinade for the lamb and blitzed it all up to a biscuity, soul-warming slather, which was then rubbed all over the lamb leg before roasting. The roasted outcome was fragrant, warming and delicious. This pared-down version is a 30-minute way of recreating that brown sugar-spiced hit of happiness.

SERVES 4

4 tbsp vegetable oil

1 onion, roughly chopped

1 cube frozen crushed garlic
   or 3 garlic cloves, crushed

1 cube frozen crushed ginger
   or 1 thumb-sized pieces fresh
   ginger, peeled and grated

4 x 200g/7oz lamb rump steaks

1 tbsp garam masala

1 tbsp ground coriander

1 tsp ground cinnamon

1 tbsp salt

1 tbsp sugar

4 ginger biscuits

1 Preheat the grill/broiler to high and line a grill pan with foil.

2 Heat 3 tablespoons of the oil in a large non-stick frying pan/skillet over a medium heat, then add the onion, garlic and ginger and cook, stirring occasionally, for 6–8 minutes, until the onions are soft and golden.

3 Meanwhile, heat the remaining tablespoon of oil in a separate frying pan over a medium heat. Add the lamb steaks and cook for 2–3 minutes on each side, until browned. Transfer the lamb steaks to the rack of a grill pan while you prepare the topping.

4 Add the garam masala, ground coriander, ground cinnamon, salt and sugar to the pan with the onions and cook, stirring continuously, for 1 minute. Tip the spiced onions into the bowl of a food processor and crumble in the ginger biscuits. Process the biscuit and onion mixture to a thick, smooth paste, then divide the mixture between the lamb steaks and spread out in an even layer.

5 Grill/broil the steaks for 4–5 minutes, until the lamb is bubbling and the paste has formed a golden crust. Serve hot.

Spiced Lamb and Apricot Wraps

In the heat of the east where meat cannot be left to hang and tenderise naturally, mincing/grinding it is the quickest and best way to make it soft and delicious. Lamb keema is always cooked with big aromatic spices that make it a very quick way to create dramatic flavours. Keema is also a wonderful vessel for any past-their-best vegetables or half-used tins that are lurking in the back of your fridge, a true more-is-more recipe.

SERVES 4

100ml/3½fl oz/scant ½ cup
   vegetable oil
2 onions, finely chopped
2 cubes frozen crushed garlic
   or 6 garlic cloves, crushed
2 cubes frozen crushed ginger
   or 2 thumb-sized pieces fresh
   ginger, peeled and grated
500g/7oz lean minced/ground lamb
200g/7oz canned chopped tomatoes
¼ tsp ground turmeric
¼ tsp chilli powder

2 tsp ground cumin
2¼ tsp garam masala
1 tsp salt
1 tsp sugar
2 tbsp pine nuts
75g/2¾oz/½ cup dried apricots,
   finely chopped
1 fat green chilli, deseeded and
   finely sliced
1 tbsp crystallised ginger, finely chopped
small handful fresh coriander/cilantro,
   roughly chopped
wraps or flatbreads, to serve

1 Heat the oil in a large pan over a medium heat, then add the onions and cook, stirring occasionally, for 6 minutes. Add the garlic and ginger to the pan and continue to cook, stirring, for another 2 minutes, until the onions are soft and just starting to turn golden.

2 Add the lamb to the pan, breaking it up with a wooden spoon as you do, and cook with the onions for 5 minutes, until browned. Add the chopped tomatoes, ground turmeric, chilli powder, ground cumin, garam masala, salt, sugar, pine nuts, apricots and 200ml/7fl oz/ generous ¾ cup of boiling water to the pan and stir to combine. Bring the mixture to the boil, then reduce the heat to a simmer and leave to cook for 10 minutes, stirring occasionally.

3 Once the lamb mixture has reduced and thickened, add the sliced chilli and crystallised ginger to the pan and stir to combine. Leave to cook for 2 minutes more, then stir through the fresh coriander/cilantro and remove the pan from the heat.

4 Transfer the lamb mixture to a serving bowl, or simply put the pan in the middle of the table, and let everyone dig in. I like to serve this with wraps for ripping off and scooping up the fragrant lamb and mopping up the juices.

Rare Spice-Rubbed Steak

I'm a huge fan of the Steak *Fiorentina* and always make a point of travelling to Florence to eat it if I am ever lucky enough to be in Italy on my holidays. There are few people in the world who unashamedly embrace their steaks in as rare and juicy a state as the Florentines. This is my version, with a little extra spice to give it that extra Mowgli kick. Be warned, you may want to have your windows open when the steak hits the pan!

SERVES 4
2 tbsp ground cumin
2 tsp salt
2 tsp garlic salt
2 tbsp paprika
1 tsp ground black pepper
4 x 225g/8oz sirloin steaks,
    at room temperature
1 tbsp vegetable oil

To serve:
80g/2¾oz rocket/arugula leaves
juice of ¼ lemon
olive oil, for drizzling
½ tsp sea salt

1 Put a large, non-stick frying pan/skillet over a high heat and leave until very hot and almost smoking.

2 While the pan is heating, put the ground cumin, salt, garlic salt, paprika and pepper on a plate and stir until well combined. Brush both sides of the steaks with the oil, then press the steaks into the spices to coat on both sides.

3 Once the pan is up to temperature, add the steaks to the pan in batches and cook for 1½–2 minutes on each side. Remove the steaks from the pan and leave to rest for 3 minutes, then slice and transfer to serving plates.

4 Divide the rocket/arugula leaves between the serving plates and drizzle with the lemon juice and a little olive oil. Sprinkle the salt over the salad, then serve.

Keema Toasties

Indians who live in geographical areas that fall under the rule of the toasted-sandwich maker do not want to feel left out. The addition of oozing, turmeric-spiced keema to the triangular toasted sandwich is a universal thread of golden assimilation that runs through the homes of Indian diaspora the world over. If you don't have a toasted-sandwich maker, you could fry the sandwiches in a hot frying pan/skillet, much like an American grilled-cheese sandwich.

SERVES 4

2 tbsp vegetable oil

1 onion, roughly chopped

2 cubes frozen crushed garlic
   or 6 garlic cloves, crushed

1 cube frozen crushed ginger
   or 1 thumb-sized piece fresh
   ginger, peeled and grated

1 tbsp garam masala

1½ tsp ground cumin

¼ tsp chilli powder

500g/1lb 2oz minced/ground lamb

200g/7oz canned chopped tomatoes

1 tsp salt

½ tsp sugar

75g/2½oz/½ cup frozen peas

1 small carrot, peeled into ribbons

1 small handful spinach

12 slices pre-sliced white bread

75g/2½oz butter

1 Heat the oil in a large, heavy-based pan over a medium-high heat. Add the onion, garlic and ginger and cook, stirring continuously, for 6–8 minutes, until the onions are golden brown.

2 Add the garam masala, ground cumin and chilli powder and stir to coat the onions in the spices, then add the lamb and cook, breaking it down with a wooden spoon and stirring to coat in the spices, until browned.

3 Tip the tomatoes into the pan along with the salt, sugar and 125ml/4fl oz/½ cup of boiling water and stir to combine. Bring the mixture to the boil, then add the peas, carrot and spinach, reduce the heat to a simmer and leave to cook, stirring occasionally, for 15 minutes.

4 While the keema is cooking, butter the bread on both sides and preheat the toasted-sandwich maker. To assemble the sandwiches, lay a slice of bread on a chopping board and spoon a quarter of the keema mixture into the centre, spreading it out in an even layer so it almost reaches the edge of the bread, but leaving a thin border, then top with another slice of bread. Repeat until you have 2–4 sandwiches assembled, depending on the size of your machine, then transfer to the toasted-sandwich maker and cook until the bread is crisp and golden brown. Keep the toasties warm while you repeat the process to use up the remaining filling and bread. Serve hot.

Last-Minute Lamb Burgers

These lamb burgers are a wonderful addition to a quickly pulled together barbecue as they are full of flavour and, providing you have lamb to hand, can be whipped up from the contents of the fridge and the spice cupboard. The pink pickled onions are great to make ahead and will live happily in your fridge for several weeks.

SERVES 4

500g/1lb 2oz minced/ground lamb
1 onion, finely chopped
1 cube frozen crushed garlic, defrosted
    or 3 garlic cloves, crushed
1½ tsp salt
1 tbsp ground cumin
¼ tsp fenugreek powder (optional)
1 tbsp finely chopped fresh mint leaves
1 fat green chilli, very finely chopped
juice of ½ lemon
½ tsp freshly ground black pepper
small bunch fresh coriander/cilantro,
    leaves very finely chopped

burger buns, mayonnaise, shredded
    lettuce and sliced tomatoes, to serve

For the pink pickled onions:

150ml/5fl oz/generous ½ cup white
    wine vinegar
50g/1¾oz/generous ¼ cup caster/
    superfine sugar
2 tsp salt
½ tsp coriander seeds
1 bay leaf
2 small red onions, halved and
    finely sliced

1 To make the pink pickled onions, put the vinegar, sugar, salt, coriander seeds and bay leaf in a small pan over a medium heat and bring just to the boil, stirring to dissolve the sugar in the liquid. Remove the pan from the heat and add the onions, then set aside to cool and pickle for at least 2 hours. These will keep in a sealed jar in the fridge for up to 2 weeks.

2 Preheat the grill/broiler to high and line a grill pan with foil, or prepare a barbecue/grill. To make the burgers, put the lamb, onion, garlic, salt, ground cumin, fenugreek powder, mint, chopped chilli, lemon juice, pepper and fresh coriander/cilantro in a large bowl and mix until well combined. Divide the mixture into 4 even-sized balls, then press those down to form patties, each slightly wider than your burger buns.

3 Cook the burgers under the grill or on the barbecue for 8–10 minutes, turning regularly until cooked to your liking.

4 To assemble the burgers, slice the buns into halves and spread each of the bases with mayonnaise. Top each with a layer of shredded lettuce, some sliced tomato and one of the burgers, then add some of the pickled onions. Cover with the bun tops, then serve.

Tandoori Lamb Chops

Everyone needs a good tandoori recipe up their sleeves. A *tandoor* is the traditional clay oven used for cooking marinated meats – the cook is swift and fierce and the meat charred and beautifully juicy, so the spices need to be big to fight through the flavour of the fire. These chops are superb under the grill/broiler, in the oven or, best of all, on the barbecue.

SERVES 4

120ml/4fl oz/½ cup vegetable oil
1 heaped tbsp tomato purée
300ml/10fl oz/1¼ cups plain yoghurt
juice of 1 lemon
1 cube frozen crushed garlic, defrosted,
    or 3 garlic cloves, crushed
2 tbsp garam masala

1 tbsp paprika
1 tsp fenugreek powder
1½ tsp salt
8 lamb chops
small handful fresh coriander/cilantro,
    leaves picked, to garnish
cooked rice, flatbreads or wraps,
    to serve

1 Preheat the grill/broiler to high and line a grill pan with foil, or prepare a barbecue.

2 Put all of the ingredients except the lamb in a large bowl and stir to combine. Add the lamb chops to the bowl and use your hands to coat them with the marinade on all sides. If you have time, you could leave these to marinate in the fridge for a few hours at this point, or they can be cooked straightaway.

3 Cook the marinated lamb chops under the grill or on the barbecue for 5–6 minutes on each side, until the meat is cooked to your liking and the edges begin to char. Serve the lamb, garnished with fresh coriander/cilantro and with your choice of rice, flatbreads or wraps alongside.

Ginger-Beer Pork

I love the bite and fragrance of ginger with pork and the addition of ginger beer in this super-simple dish makes it the work of moments. The sweetness that the ginger beer brings is also wonderful when offset with the pungent, savoury hit of the English mustard. You could use wholegrain or Dijon if you prefer, both of which would give a slightly tart edge to the dish that would also be very welcome.

SERVES 4

3 tbsp vegetable oil
1 clove garlic, crushed
4 pork loin medallions
½ tsp salt
½ tsp ground black pepper

150ml/5fl oz/generous ½ cup
  ginger beer
1 heaped tsp English mustard
150ml/5fl oz/generous ½ cup
  crème fraîche
2 tbsp chopped fresh parsley, to garnish

1 Heat the oil in a large frying pan/skillet over a medium heat, then add the garlic and cook for 1 minute, stirring and being careful not to let it burn. Add the pork to the pan and cook for 3 minutes on each side, until golden.

2 Season the pork with the salt and pepper, then pour over the ginger beer and add the mustard. Give everything a stir, then add the crème fraîche and stir again to combine. Cook for 2–3 minutes, until the sauce thickens and reduces slightly. Divide the pork medallions between serving plates and spoon over the sauce. Serve the pork garnished with the chopped parsley and with your choice of cooked vegetables alongside.

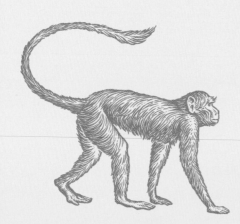

Spinach Meatball Curry

This simple curry of spiced meatballs bobbing around in a fragrant sauce is much-loved in my house. I always have spinach that needs using up in my fridge and curries such as this are tremendous at hiding it under a robe of distracting and delicious flavour and texture from veg-dodging children.

SERVES 4

100ml/3½fl oz/scant ½ cup
    vegetable oil
2 onions, roughly chopped
2 cubes frozen crushed ginger
    or 2 thumb-sized pieces fresh
    ginger, peeled and grated
2 cubes frozen crushed garlic
    or 6 garlic cloves, crushed
3 tbsp garam masala
¼ tsp chilli powder
1 tsp ground turmeric
1 tsp salt

1 tsp sugar
400g/14oz canned chopped tomatoes
80g/3oz baby spinach leaves
cooked rice, to serve
1 handful fresh coriander/cilantro,
    leaves and stems chopped, to garnish

For the meatballs:

500g/1lb 2oz lean minced/
    ground lamb
1 tbsp ground cumin
1 tbsp ground coriander
1 tsp salt

1 Heat the oil in a large, heavy-based pan over a medium-high heat. Add the onions and cook, stirring occasionally, for 6 minutes, until soft and translucent. Add the garlic and ginger and cook, stirring, for a further 2 minutes, until the onions have started to turn golden brown.

2 While the onions are cooking, put all the ingredients for the meatballs in a large bowl and mix with your hands until well combined. Set aside.

3 Add the garam masala, chilli powder and ground turmeric to the pan with the onions and stir to combine, then tip in the salt, sugar, chopped tomatoes and 400ml/14fl oz/scant 1¾ cups of boiling water and stir again until well combined. Bring the mixture to a boil, then reduce the heat to a lively simmer and leave to bubble away while you make the meatballs.

4 Take a heaped teaspoon of the meatball mixture and roll in your hands to form a small meatball. Set aside and repeat the process until all of the meat is used up.

5 Drop the meatballs into the simmering sauce and stir to coat the meat in the sauce. Leave to cook for 10 minutes, then stir through the spinach and cook for 5 minutes more.

6 Divide the curry between serving plates or bowl and serve garnished with fresh coriander/cilantro and with cooked rice alongside.

Sumac Lamb Steaks

Sumac is a great ingredient for bringing an interesting floral tang to heavy meat and oily fish, and these steaks have the acreage to show off its beautiful flavour. I've suggested serving these with a salad for a light meal, but potatoes would always be welcome!

SERVES 4

2 tbsp olive oil
1 clove garlic, crushed
1 tsp salt
finely grated zest of 1 lemon
2 tbsp sumac
4 lamb leg steaks
salad, to serve

1 Preheat the grill/broiler to high and line a grill pan with foil.

2 Put the oil, garlic, salt, lemon zest and the sumac in a bowl and mix to combine. Brush the lamb steaks with the mixture on both sides, then lay on the prepared grill pan.

3 Grill/broil the steaks for 4–5 minutes on each side, until golden brown and beginning to char.

4 Leave the steaks to rest for a few minutes, then serve hot with you choice of salad alongside.

83

MEAT

After-School Pepper Pot

This is standard after-school fare for many Hungarian children. In Hungary it is known as *Letcho* and is extremely popular. It is fragrant and tangy and uses heaps of naturally sweet peppers, so is great for sneaking an extra portion of veg into the kids. Better still, and the reason I make it so often, is because it is a great way of using up leftover cooked rice.

SERVES 4

150g/5½oz/scant 1 cup basmati rice

2 tbsp olive oil

225g/8oz chorizo, cut into
   1cm/½in cubes

1 onion, roughly chopped

1 cube frozen crushed garlic
   or 3 garlic cloves, crushed

1 tbsp paprika

1 tsp ground turmeric

freshly ground black pepper

4 peppers of any colour, deseeded
   and cut into bite-sized chunks

800g/1lb 12oz canned chopped
   tomatoes

1 tbsp sugar

1 tsp salt

1 chicken stock cube, crumbled

1 Bring a large pan of water to the boil over a high heat. Pour in the rice, stir once, then reduce the heat to a simmer and cook, according to packet instructions, until tender. Drain and set aside until needed.

2 Heat the oil in a large pan over a medium heat, add the chorizo and cook, stirring, for 1 minute to release the oils, then add the onion and garlic and cook for 2 minutes, stirring, until softened. Add the paprika, ground turmeric and a few grinds of black pepper to the pan and stir to combine with the onions, then add the peppers, chopped tomatoes, sugar, salt and the crumbled stock cube, and stir again. Add the cooked rice to the pan and stir to combine, then leave to cook, stirring occasionally, for 10 minutes, until the sauce has thickened and the peppers are tender. Serve hot.

Ten-Minute, Late-Night Kebabs

Opening the fridge and gazing into its comforting light after a long day can soothe the soul but also be a torment if nothing immediately jumps out to sate your hunger. If you chance upon a packet of minced/ground lamb in there, these kebabs are effortless but utterly satisfying. You can serve them in wraps, with chips or on their own. However you choose, they will be delicious.

SERVES 4

500g/1lb 2oz minced/ground lamb
1 fat green chilli, finely chopped
1 onion, finely chopped
juice of 1 lemon
1 clove garlic, crushed
½ tsp salt
2 tbsp ground cumin
small handful fresh coriander/cilantro, leaves finely chopped

1 red onion, halved and finely sliced, to serve
tortilla wraps, to serve

For the mint yoghurt:

100ml/3½fl oz/scant ½ cup Greek yoghurt
2 tbsp mint jelly

1 Preheat the grill/broiler to high and line a grill pan with foil.

2 Put the lamb, chopped chilli, onion, lemon juice, garlic, salt, ground cumin and 2 tablespoons of the fresh coriander/cilantro in a large bowl and use your hands to mix until everything is really well combined.

3 Divide the mixture into 8 equal-sized balls, then form each ball into a sausage shape, each around 6cm/2½in long. Lay the kofta on the prepared grill pan and grill/broil for 6–8 minutes, turning regularly, until golden and cooked through.

4 While the kofta are cooking, put the yoghurt and mint jelly in a bowl and stir to combine.

5 Once cooked, serve the kofta in the middle of the table, passing the wraps, mint yoghurt and sliced red onions around for everyone to assemble their own kebabs.

Wild Garlic and Lamb Salad

This is a wonderful spring salad when the lamb is at its best and fragrant wild garlic is abundant. Its heft comes from the combination of nutty, creamy potatoes and the sharp spiced lamb. If you can't get wild garlic, chopped spinach leaves work perfectly well. The pears, however, add an unexpected sweet refrain that can't be replaced.

SERVES 4

500g/1lb 2oz new potatoes

400g/14oz lamb leg steaks, cut into bite-sized chunks

1 tbsp ground cumin

1 tbsp amchoor

1 tsp garlic purée

1 tsp salt

2 tbsp olive oil

1 tbsp butter

1 tsp salt

small handful fresh coriander/cilantro, leaves roughly chopped

handful wild garlic or spinach, roughly chopped

2 large pears, chopped or cut into wedges, skin on

juice of ½ lemon

1 Put the potatoes in a large pan and add cold, salted water to cover. Put the pan over a high heat and bring to the boil, then reduce to a simmer and cook for 15–20 minutes, until the potatoes are tender.

2 Meanwhile, put the lamb in a bowl with the ground cumin, amchoor, garlic purée and salt and stir to coat the meat well in the spices.

3 Heat 1 tablespoon of the oil in a large, non-stick frying pan/skillet over a medium heat, then add the lamb and cook, stirring continuously, for around 5 minutes, until it is golden brown and beginning to char around the edges. Remove from the heat and set aside.

4 Drain the potatoes through a colander and leave to steam dry for a couple of minutes, then return to the pan and toss with the remaining tablespoon of oil and the butter. Transfer the potatoes to a large bowl and add the fresh coriander/cilantr`o, wild garlic or spinach, and pears. Give everything a mix to combine, then add the cooked lamb to the bowl and pour over the lemon juice. Toss everything again, then spoon the salad into serving bowls and serve immediately.

Minced Pork and Glass Noodle Broth

I have a great fondness for these Korean-style soups that are abundant with punchy herbs, flavour and texture, and I especially love the way the glass noodles yield their elastic charm when you drop them into the soup. I add minced/ground pork to this but you can change that for tofu or bean-curd sheets if you prefer, both of which are equally capable of adding interest and texture.

SERVES 4

120ml/4fl oz/½ cup vegetable oil

2 cubes frozen crushed garlic
    or 6 garlic cloves, crushed

2 cubes frozen crushed ginger
    or 2 thumb-sized pieces fresh
    ginger, peeled and grated

1 fat green chilli, sliced

1 bunch spring onions/scallions,
    white and green parts finely sliced

125g/4½oz broccoli or green beans,
    cut into bite-sized pieces

400g/14oz minced/ground pork

1 tsp black pepper

1 tbsp sugar

4 tbsp light soy sauce

4 tbsp shaoxing rice wine

2 tbsp fish sauce

3 chicken stock cubes, crumbled

100g/3½oz dried glass noodles

small bunch coriander/cilantro,
    leaves and stalks chopped

½ bunch mint, leaves picked
    and chopped

1 tbsp sesame oil

1 Heat the oil in a large pan over a medium heat, then add the garlic, ginger, sliced chilli and the white part of the spring onions/scallions and cook, stirring continuously, for 3 minutes. Add the broccoli or green beans to the pan and cook, still stirring, for 2 minutes to coat in the oil and spices.

2 Add the pork to pan, breaking it down with a wooden spoon and cook, stirring continuously, until browned, then stir through the pepper, sugar, soy sauce, rice wine and fish sauce and leave to bubble away for 2 minutes.

3 Pour 2l/3½ pints/generous 8 cups of boiling water into the pan and crumble in the stock cubes. Give the mixture a stir to combine, then reduce the heat to a simmer and add the glass noodles to the pan. Cook the noodles in the mixture for 5 minutes, until tender. As the noodles start to soften, use kitchen scissors to snip them into shorter lengths in the pan.

4 Once the noodles are tender, stir the fresh coriander/cilantro, mint leaves and green part of the spring onions through the broth. Ladle the mixture into serving bowls and drizzle each bowl with a little of the sesame oil. Serve hot.

3
FISH

I'm from an area of India that is laced with rivers and, as a Bengali, my culinary mind is dominated by fish dishes. As such, this chapter could have gone on forever so I have had to employ all my restraint.

Some of my earliest memories are of going to the early morning fish market in Varanasi with my grandmother and being surrounded by all that glistened. I was taught to look for pink gills and clear eyes and remember the smell being sweet, almost floral. Back in the 1970s we didn't have a fridge in our ancestral home and so fish was always served for lunch before it could perish in the heat of the sun.

In lieu of play dates and plastic toys, I was taught the thrill of descaling and preparing sweet, pink-fleshed fish in big copper vats of water on my grandmother's veranda.

In this chapter I have given you a few Indian classics but the rest of them are dishes that I have conjured up as, in adulthood, I continue to spend my days enjoying playing with the fruits of the sea above all other ingredients.

Bengali Fish Curry

This is one of my favourite dishes. So much so that when the women in my family gathered around me to cook for me before my wedding day, as is tradition, this is what I requested. I've opted for boneless white fish fillets here, but traditionally it is cooked with the very bony but delicious *Hilsa* fish, and you can always spot a true Bengali by the way they can navigate their way around the bones!

SERVES 4

600g/1lb 5oz haddock or cod loin, skin on, cut into 5cm/2in pieces
3½ tbsp vegetable oil
1¼ tsp salt
2 tsp ground turmeric
½ tsp nigella seeds
1 fat green chilli, pierced a few times with a knife
1 tsp ground coriander
¼ tsp chilli powder
4 heaped tbsp plain yoghurt
½ tbsp English mustard
juice of ½ lemon
small bunch fresh coriander/cilantro, leaves and stems chopped
1 tbsp mustard oil, to garnish
cooked rice, to serve

1 Put the haddock or cod loin in a bowl with 1½ tablespoons of the vegetable oil, ¼ teaspoon of salt and 1 teaspoon of the ground turmeric. Use your hands to mix well, ensuring the fish is well coated in the oil and turmeric. Set aside.

2 Heat the remaining 2 tablespoons of oil in a large, non-stick pan over a medium-high heat. Add the nigella seeds and cook, stirring, until they start to pop, then add the whole green chilli, ground coriander, chilli powder and remaining teaspoon of ground turmeric, and stir to combine the spices.

3 Reduce the heat to low, then stir the yoghurt through the spice mixture in the pan. (Don't worry if the yoghurt splits at this stage.) Add the remaining teaspoon of salt and 300ml/10fl oz/1¼ cups of boiling water and stir through until everything is well combined. Bring the mixture to a simmer, then add the mustard and stir the sauce again to combine. Add the turmeric-coated fish to the pan and stir to combine with the sauce, then leave to cook at a gentle simmer for 6–8 minutes, until the fish is cooked through.

4 Remove the pan from the heat and add the lemon juice, to taste. Stir through the fresh coriander/cilantro and spoon the curry onto serving plates with rice alongside. Drizzle a little mustard oil over each serving of curry before serving.

Gin and Tonic Salmon

This dish was born when, in a moment of inspiration, I poured my glass of gin and tonic onto my marinating salmon steaks and baked them, wondering what alchemy it would perform. They were stunning. The botanicals in the gin bring a high floral note and the tonic, believe it or not, brings an open-hearted honey to this light and elegant sauce. If you have the foresight to marinade them the night before, they are pretty much cured by morning and just need a final flash of heat to finish.

SERVES 4

2 tbsp olive oil

2 x 250ml/9fl oz tins ready-mixed gin and tonic, or 500ml/18fl oz/ generous 2 cups gin and tonic, how you like it

1 tbsp ground coriander

juice of 1 lemon

1 tbsp salt

½ tsp black pepper

2 cubes frozen crushed garlic, defrosted or 6 cloves garlic, crushed

4 skin-on salmon fillets

1 tbsp chopped fresh coriander/cilantro, to garnish

steamed seasonal vegetables, to serve

1 Preheat the oven to 180°C/350°F/gas mark 4.

2 In the base of a large roasting tin, combine the olive oil, gin and tonic, ground coriander, lemon juice, salt, pepper and garlic, stirring until well combined. Lay the salmon in the sauce, skin-side up, then cover the dish with foil and transfer to the oven for 20 minutes, until the salmon is cooked through, but still slightly translucent in the centre.

3 Remove the salmon from the tin and set aside, then place the tin over a medium heat, bring to the boil and cook until reduced by half. Divide the salmon fillets between serving plates and spoon over the sauce. Serve the salmon scattered with fresh coriander/cilantro and with steamed, seasonal vegetables alongside.

Ginger and Garlic Mussels with Lime Leaves

Good mussels don't need many ingredients to make them sing. Instead of the knee-jerk response of cooking them in white wine, these Thai flavours ask a very different question. I love them.

SERVES 4

2 tbsp vegetable oil
1 small onion, finely chopped
2 cubes frozen crushed garlic
    or 6 garlic cloves, crushed
2 cubes frozen crushed ginger
    or 2 thumb-sized pieces fresh
    ginger, peeled and grated
1 fat green chilli, sliced

¼ tsp ground turmeric
1½kg/3lbs 5oz fresh mussels,
    cleaned and beards removed
4 kaffir lime leaves
400ml/14fl oz canned coconut milk
zest and juice of 1 lime
small bunch fresh coriander/cilantro,
    roughly chopped

1 Heat the oil in a large pan over a medium-high heat. Add the onion, garlic, ginger and sliced chilli and cook for 4 minutes, stirring continuously, until the onion is soft and translucent. Add the ground turmeric, mussels, lime leaves and coconut milk and give the pan a careful shake to combine. Cover with a lid and leave to cook for 5–6 minutes, until the mussels have steamed open.

2 Remove the lid from the pan and stir through lime zest and juice and the chopped coriander/cilantro. Ladle the mussels and their fragrant broth into serving bowls and serve hot.

Curry House Prawn and Mushroom Omelette

Eggs are a popular ingredient in the Indian kitchen, as they go a long way and are a great blank canvas for all kinds of spices and additions. There is a pillowy charm to an omelette that brings a level of comfort that few other dishes afford – it might be for this reason that there is often a late-night rush on omelette orders at my local curry house. Here the comfort factor is levelled up even further with the addition of soft prawns/shrimp and even softer mushrooms, but the underlying kick from the spices and fresh chilli give this nursery food a grown-up edge.

SERVES 4

4 tsp vegetable oil
¼ tsp nigella seeds
1 clove garlic, crushed
80g/3oz cooked king prawns/ jumbo shrimp
4 chestnut/cremini mushrooms, sliced
8 large eggs
½ tsp salt
1 small onion, finely chopped
1 fat green chilli, deseeded and finely chopped
2 tbsp chopped fresh coriander/ cilantro leaves
1 tsp ground coriander
1 tsp ground cumin

1 Preheat the grill/broiler to high.

2 Heat the oil in a 24cm/9½in frying pan/skillet over a medium heat. Add the nigella seeds and cook, stirring, until they begin to pop, then immediately add the garlic, prawns/shrimp and mushrooms and continue to cook for another 2 minutes.

3 Crack the eggs into a large bowl and beat to combine, then add the salt, onion, chilli, fresh coriander/cilantro, ground coriander and ground cumin and beat again until all the ingredients are well incorporated.

4 Pour the egg mixture into the pan over the prawns and mushrooms, ensuring that all of the elements are evenly spread across the pan and leave to cook for 8–9 minutes, until the omelette is set at the edges but still has some wobble in the centre.

5 Place the pan under the preheated grill for 2–3 minutes, until the surface of the omelette is puffed and golden brown. Slide the omelette out of the pan onto a plate or board and cut into slices. Serve hot, with wraps alongside.

Prawn and Broccoli Curry

Cooked prawns/shrimp and tender broccoli cook so quickly and work wonderfully together in this fresh and tangy curry. The sauce at the base of this dish is spiced with *panch phoron*, a Bengali five-spice mixture, which is the mother of ingredient resurrection. The spice, tomato and mustard marry together perfectly, and it makes a wonderful vehicle for whatever you might want to use up from your fridge.

SERVES 4

5 tbsp vegetable oil

2 fat green chillies, pierced with a sharp knife

1 tbsp panch phoron

150g/5oz broccoli, head cut into small florets, stalk sliced

200g/7oz canned chopped tomatoes

¼ tsp chilli powder

1 tsp ground turmeric

300g/10½oz cooked king prawns/ jumbo shrimp

1 heaped tbsp English mustard

½ tsp salt

1 tsp sugar

1 small bunch fresh coriander/cilantro, roughly chopped

juice of ½ lemon

1 Heat 3½ tablespoons of the oil in a large pan over a high heat. Add the whole chillies and panch phoron and fry for 10 seconds, stirring, then reduce the heat to low and add the broccoli, chopped tomatoes, chilli powder, ½ teaspoon of the ground turmeric and 250ml/ 9fl oz/scant 1 cup of water. Stir to combine, then bring the mixture to a simmer and cook for 10–12 minutes, until the broccoli is tender.

2 Meanwhile, put the remaining 1½ tablespoons of oil and ½ teaspoon of turmeric in a bowl with the prawns and toss to combine. Place a frying pan over a medium-high heat, then add the prawns and cook, stirring continuously for 2 minutes.

3 Tip the cooked prawns into the curry along with the mustard, salt and sugar, stir to combine, then cook the curry for another 3 minutes. Remove from the heat, scatter over the chopped coriander/cilantro and drizzle with the lemon juice. Serve hot with your choice of cooked rice and flatbreads alongside.

Indian Fish Finger Sandwich

This dish is an ode to my mother's ability to meddle. When we first discovered McDonald's in the UK in 1978, we would drive all the way to London for a Filet-O-Fish. In the back of our Ford Anglia, Ma would open her handbag and produce some homemade green chilli pickle and finely sliced red onion and set to work on her hard-won prize. As children, we were always mortified, but it turns out that mothers really do know best.

SERVES 4
vegetable oil, for frying
125g/4½oz/1 cup gram/chickpea
    flour, plus extra for sprinkling
½ tsp salt
1 tsp baking powder
½ tsp ground turmeric
⅛ tsp chilli powder
½ tsp ajwain seeds
1 tsp white poppy seeds
350g/12oz white fish fillets (haddock
    or cod work well), cut into 12 goujons
8 slices white bread, buttered

For the gherkin and coriander raita:
250g/9oz/scant 2½ cups Greek
    yoghurt
juice of ¼ lemon
½ tsp ground cumin
½ clove garlic, crushed
½ tsp salt
2 tbsp roughly chopped gherkins
small handful fresh coriander/cilantro,
    roughly chopped

1 Following manufacturers' guidelines, add oil to a deep-fat fryer and preheat to 180°C/350°F/gas mark 4. If you don't have a deep-fat dryer, simply put 4cm/1½in of vegetable oil in the base of a large pan and set over a medium-high heat.

2 Sift the flour into a large bowl and add the salt, baking powder, ground turmeric, chilli powder, ajwain seeds and poppy seeds and stir to combine. Make a well in the centre and gradually whisk in around 150ml/5fl oz/generous ½ cup of cold water to make a thick batter.

3 Check the oil by carefully dropping in a small spoonful of batter into it – if the batter bubbles and floats to the surface then it is ready. Sprinkle the fish goujons with a little flour, then dip them into the batter to cover, shaking off any excess. Carefully lower the coated goujons into the oil and fry for 3–4 minutes, until the batter is puffed and golden and the fish is cooked through. Set aside while you prepare the rest of the elements.

4 To make the raita, put all the ingredients in a bowl and mix until well combined.

5 Spread each of the bread slices with some of the raita. Lay the goujons over half of the bread slices, then top the sandwiches with the remaining bread. Cut into halves and enjoy!

Tamarind Salmon Curry

This is my nod to the wonderment of South-Indian fish curries. To make it accessible, I brought the chilli right down in this dish, but I did want to quickly recreate that uniquely tamarind tangy wake-up call that you can only get from a golden Goan beach shack fish-curry breakfast. Yum.

SERVES 4

150ml/5fl oz/generous ½ cup vegetable oil

2 tsp mustard seeds

1 tsp cumin seeds

1 dried red chilli

1 onion, halved and thinly sliced

2 cubes frozen crushed garlic or 6 garlic cloves, crushed

2 cubes frozen crushed ginger or 2 thumb-sized pieces fresh root ginger, peeled and grated

600g/1lb 5oz skinless salmon fillet, cut into bite-sized pieces

½ tsp ground turmeric

400g/14oz canned chopped tomatoes

¼ tsp chilli powder

2 tsp tamarind concentrate

3 tbsp brown sugar

1 tsp salt

small bunch fresh coriander/cilantro, leaves and stalks chopped, to garnish

cooked rice, flatbreads or rice, to serve

1 Heat 100ml/3½fl oz of the oil in a large pan over a high heat, then add the mustard and cumin seeds and fry, stirring, until they start to pop and turn grey. Reduce the heat to medium, then add the dried chilli, onion, garlic and ginger and cook, stirring occasionally, for 8 minutes, until the onions are soft and translucent.

2 Meanwhile, put the salmon in a bowl with the ground turmeric and use your hands to coat the fish. Heat the remaining oil in a separate pan over a medium heat, then add the salmon and fry for 1–2 minutes on each side to seal. Remove from the heat and set aside.

3 Add the chopped tomatoes to the pan with the onions and stir to combine. Bring the mixture to a boil then reduce to a simmer and leave to cook, stirring occasionally, for 6 minutes, until thick and reduced. Add the chilli powder, tamarind concentrate, sugar, salt and 400ml/14fl oz/1⅔ cups of water and stir to combine. Bring to a simmer, then leave to cook for 6–8 minutes, until the salmon is tender. Scatter over the coriander/cilantro and serve hot with your choice of rice or flatbreads alongside.

108

Mango and Coriander Salmon

I love this dish. The fact that it's super simple and that the magic at the heart of it comes from opening a tin of mango slices makes me even more proud of how achievable and truly delicious it is. It also works brilliantly with tinned gooseberries or rhubarb in lieu of the mango, if you prefer tart to sweet.

SERVES 4

2 tbsp vegetable oil, plus 150ml/
    5fl oz/generous ½ cup, for frying
¼ tsp cumin seeds
½ clove garlic, crushed
425g/15oz tinned mango slices
1 tbsp ground coriander
1 tsp salt

juice of ½ lemon
¼ tsp chilli powder
100g/3½oz/¾ cup plain/all-purpose
    flour
4 skinless salmon fillets (approx.
    125g/4½oz each)
cooked rice, flatbreads or wraps,
    to serve

1 Heat 2 tablespoons of the vegetable oil in a large pan over a medium heat. Add the cumin seeds and garlic and fry, stirring, for 30 seconds. Pour the tin of mango slices, including the syrup, into the pan, then add the ground coriander, salt, lemon juice and chilli powder. Using a fork, mash the mango into the spices, then cook the mixture, stirring occasionally, for 5 minutes, until you have a slightly pulpy paste. Remove the pan from the heat and set aside to cool a little.

2 Sift the flour onto a plate and set on the kitchen counter next to the pan of mango mixture. Dip the salmon fillets first in the mango paste, to coat, then roll in the flour. Set aside and decant the remaining mango sauce into a serving bowl.

3 Put the remaining 150ml/5fl oz/generous ½ cup of oil in a large pan and set over a medium heat. Once hot, carefully add the salmon fillets and cook for 3–4 minutes on each side, until a golden crust has formed and the salmon has cooked through. Serve the salmon hot, with the remaining mango sauce alongside to spoon over. This is lovely served with rice or with wraps alongside for mopping up the sauce.

4

VEGETABLES
AND PULSES

It's very often vegetables that dominate the leftover scene in the fridge. This is probably because meat has a firm use-by date and an associated anxiety with not letting it slip past that point. By contrast, it's often the case that I open the fridge and will find quarter of a red pepper, half a cabbage, a shrivelling leek, a few sticks of floppy celery or some past-their-best beans languishing at the bottom of the veg drawer.

What I love about these ingredients is that I could come in from a two-week holiday and within 45 minutes could easily have three or four dishes on the table. They are the Dad's Army of kitchen ingredients – stalwart, dormant and ready to spring into life-saving, colourful rescue.

114

It's not in my nature to simply steam and butter vegetables, as glorious as that can be. In the Indian kitchen you are raised to understand that certain vegetables are dressed with certain spices. And who am I to challenge that?

It is some of those backbone, go-to dishes that I have given you in this chapter. They are not bridesmaid support dishes to a main meat act, and though you could happily serve them as part of a feast, they are designed to be completely standalone and satisfying in their own right. They are gorgeous with flatbreads, rice or, indeed, with couscous, quinoa or bulgur wheat – whatever your cupboards yield in your search for sustenance.

Million-Dollar Dahl

In Eastern Europe it is tradition at New Year to have these whole lentil dishes. I add a little more spice than my mother-in-law's original recipe calls for, but the extra oomph really works. The green discs of lentil represent little coins and a wish for wealth in the year ahead. This is a wonderful centrepiece to a meal, regardless of your guests needs, as it is both gluten-free and vegan, as well as filling and delicious.

SERVES 4

4 tbsp vegetable oil

1 tsp cumin seeds

1 onion, roughly chopped

1 cube frozen crushed garlic
  or 3 garlic cloves, crushed

2 cubes frozen crushed ginger
  or 2 thumb-sized pieces fresh
  ginger, peeled and grated

1 bay leaf

1 fat green chilli, sliced

800g /1lb 12oz canned green
  lentils, drained

1 tsp ground turmeric

1 tbsp garam masala

1 tsp ground cumin

400g/14oz canned chopped tomatoes

1½ tsp salt

small handful fresh coriander/cilantro,
  roughly chopped

1 Heat the oil in a large pan over a medium heat, then add the cumin seeds and fry for a few seconds, until they are fragrant and have turned a deep golden brown. Add the onion, garlic, ginger, bay leaf and sliced chilli, and cook, stirring occasionally, for about 8 minutes, until the onions are soft and golden.

2 Add the lentils, ground turmeric, garam masala, ground cumin and chopped tomatoes to the pan and stir to combine. Bring to the boil, then reduce the heat to a lively simmer and cook for 20 minutes, adding a splash of water if the mixture gets too dry, until the lentils are tender. Add the salt to the pan to taste, then stir through the chopped fresh coriander/cilantro. Serve hot.

Courgette and Cashew Curry

What I love about this curry is that it is cooked with pickling spices, so it is brilliant when it is hot and fresh but also fantastic served cold and fermented. If you have any leftover, it is wonderful in toasted sandwiches or as a pickled, cold accompaniment to cooked meats.

SERVES 4

4 tbsp vegetable oil
½ tsp fenugreek seeds
1 tsp asafoetida
1 dried red chill, crumbled
4 courgettes/zucchini (approx. 800g/
   1lb 12oz), halved lengthways then
   cut into 2cm/¾in pieces
½ tsp ground turmeric
¼ tsp chilli powder
1 tsp salt
1 tsp sugar
100g/3½oz/scant 1 cup
   unsalted cashew nuts
squeeze of lemon
wraps, to serve

1 Heat the oil in a large, non-stick frying pan over a medium heat. Add the fenugreek seeds and fry for a few seconds, until fragrant and just turning golden, then add the asafoetida and dried, crumbled red chilli and fry for a few seconds more, being careful not to burn any of the spices as this will impart a bitter taste to the curry.

2 Add the courgettes/zucchini, ground turmeric, chilli powder, salt and sugar, and stir to combine the vegetables with the spices. Then add the cashew nuts and stir again. Bring the mixture to the boil, then reduce the heat to a simmer and leave to cook, stirring occasionally, for 20 minutes, until the courgettes are tender. Add lemon juice, to taste, then serve the curry hot, with wraps alongside for scooping.

118

Super-Simple Tomato and Nigella Soup

Soup isn't part of the Indian culinary language but there is something so wholesome about it, and because it is not something I learned at my mother's knee, I always feel so clever when I make it from scratch. I know that the ease and nursery appeal of canned, ready-made tomato soup is hard to beat, but this is sublime and can be made for a fraction of the cost, plus it's completely free from any preservatives or any of those hidden ingredients that didn't come from your own heart. I add butter/lima beans to give the body of the soup a bit more heft, but you could leave them out if you prefer. The perfect balance of sweet and salty in tomato soup is unique to everyone – I like mine quite sweet, but you may not – so keep tasting and adjust the seasoning to suit your tastes.

SERVES 4

2 tbsp olive oil

1 tsp nigella seeds

1 cube frozen crushed garlic
   or 3 garlic cloves, crushed

1.2kg/2lbs 6oz canned chopped
   tomatoes

400g/7oz canned butter/lima beans,
   drained

3 ham or chicken stock cubes, crumbled

1 tsp ground turmeric

4 tbsp sugar, or to taste

salt, to taste

2 tbsp crème fraîche, optional

crusty bread, to serve

1 Heat the oil in a large pan over a medium heat, then add the nigella seeds and cook, stirring, for 2 minutes. Add the garlic and cook, stirring, for 1 minute, until fragrant, then add the chopped tomatoes, butter/lima beans, stock cubes, ground turmeric, sugar and 300ml/10fl oz/1¼ cups of boiling water and stir to combine. Bring the mixture to the boil, then reduce the heat to a simmer and leave to cook for 10–12 minutes, until slightly thickened.

2 Remove the pan from the heat and use a stick/immersion blender to blend until smooth. Taste the soup and adjust the seasoning as required. If you prefer a creamier soup, stir through the crème fraîche, otherwise leave it out or serve it alongside for everyone to add their own. Spoon the soup into serving bowls and serve hot with crusty bread alongside for dipping.

Cauliflower, Sugar Snap and Almond Curry

The secret to a good cauliflower curry is to hold your nerve and not add water. The slow and gentle steamy cooking is really important, as is cutting cauliflower into small florets. If the cauliflower is cut too large, it simply won't cook and will completely exasperate you. Follow the instructions and you can't go wrong.

SERVES 4

4 tbsp vegetable oil
1 tsp cumin seeds
1 fat green chilli, pierced
  a few times with a knife
8 new potatoes
1 cauliflower, head cut into
  small florets, stalk chopped
1 tsp salt

½ tsp ground turmeric
2 tsp ground coriander
1/8 tsp chilli powder
1 tsp sugar
150g/5½oz sugar snaps
25g/1oz flaked almonds
squeeze of lemon juice
cooked rice or flatbreads, to serve

1 Heat the oil in a large pan over a medium-high heat. Add the cumin seeds and fry until fragrant and deep golden brown. Add the whole chilli to the pan and cook, stirring, for around 30 seconds, until the skin is blistered all over. Reduce the heat to low, then add the potatoes and the chopped stalk from the cauliflower and cook, stirring occasionally, for 6 minutes, until just starting to soften.

2 Add the cauliflower florets, salt, ground turmeric, ground coriander, chilli powder and sugar and stir to combine the vegetables with the spices. Cover the pan with a lid and leave to cook for 5 minutes, stirring occasionally, then add the sugar snaps, cover again, and cook for another 5 minutes, stirring occasionally, until all the vegetables are tender. This is a dry curry and the veg should sweat themselves cooked, rather than simmering away in a sauce, so try and hold your nerve and don't panic if the mixture looks dry, though you can add a tiny splash of water to the pan if you are really concerned.

3 While the curry is cooking, toast the almonds in a small frying pan/skillet over a medium heat, until golden.

4 Once the curry is cooked, add lemon juice, to taste, and gently fold through the flaked almonds. Serve hot, with your choice of rice or flatbreads alongside.

122

Spinach and Chickpea Curry

It is these kind of lob-in-a-pan-and-make-magic dishes that are packed with flavour and yet can be conjured up in minutes from sleeping ingredients that I find particularly satisfying. This one also has the added benefit of being meat and dairy free, so is perfect for having on standby if you ever find yourself entertaining a hungry vegan at short notice.

SERVES 4

4 tbsp vegetable oil

1½ tsp cumin seeds

2 bay leaves

1 onion, finely chopped

2 cubes frozen crushed garlic
   or 6 garlic cloves, crushed

2 cubes frozen crushed ginger
   or 2 thumb-sized pieces fresh
   ginger, peeled and grated

2 tbsp garam masala

½ tsp chilli powder

1½ tsp ground turmeric

50g/1¾oz creamed coconut

400g/14oz canned chopped tomatoes

400g/14oz canned chickpeas/
   garbanzo beans, drained and rinsed

400g/14oz canned spinach, drained
   or 200g/7oz frozen spinach

1½ tsp salt

1 tsp sugar

1 small bunch fresh coriander/cilantro,
   roughly chopped

cooked rice or flatbreads, to serve

1 Heat the oil in a large pan over a medium-high heat, then add the cumin seeds and fry for a few seconds until fragrant and deep golden brown. Reduce the heat to medium, then add the bay leaves, onion, garlic and ginger, and cook, stirring occasionally, for around 8 minutes, until the onions are soft and golden.

2 Add the garam masala, chilli powder and ground turmeric and stir to combine, then continue to cook for 2 minutes, until the spices are fragrant. Add the creamed coconut, chopped tomatoes, chickpeas/garbanzo beans, spinach, salt and sugar to the pan and stir to combine. Bring the mixture to a boil, then reduce the heat to a simmer and leave to cook for 15 minutes. Stir through the chopped coriander/cilantro, then spoon into serving bowls and serve hot, with rice or flatbreads alongside.

Spiced Butter Bean Curry

For convenience and heft, you can't beat a butter/lima bean, and I would wholeheartedly recommend adding a couple of tins to your regular weekly shop. In any of my curry recipes that call for meat, you can happily substitute butter beans, which absorb flavours and juices so well and have the bonus of living dormant at the back of the storecupboard waiting to be called on. They are truly one of the most biddable, useful and hardworking ingredients in your kitchen. This dish is really tangy and beautiful – as if the classic Greek baked-bean dish *Plaki* has just returned from a backpacking trip to the exotic heat of the East.

SERVES 4

125ml/4fl oz/½ cup vegetable oil
2 onions, roughly chopped
2 cubes frozen crushed garlic
    or 6 garlic cloves, crushed
2 cubes frozen crushed ginger
    or 2 thumb-sized pieces fresh
    ginger, peeled and grated
1 tbsp garam masala
1 tbsp ground coriander
1 tsp ground cumin
½ tsp ground cinnamon

¼ tsp chilli powder
1 tsp ground turmeric
400g/14oz canned chopped tomatoes
2 bay leaves
800g/1lb 12oz canned butter/lima
    beans, drained
1½ tsp salt
1 tsp sugar
1 tsp English mustard
small handful coriander/cilantro,
    roughly chopped

127

1 Heat the oil in a large pan over a medium heat, then add the onions, garlic and ginger, and cook, stirring occasionally, for 8 minutes, until the onions are soft and golden. Stir the garam masala, ground coriander, ground cumin, ground cinnamon, chilli powder and ground turmeric through the onions, then add the chopped tomatoes, bay leaves, butter/lima beans, salt, sugar and 400ml/14fl oz/scant 1¾ cups of water and stir to combine. Bring the mixture to a boil, then reduce the heat to a lively simmer and cook for 15 minutes, until the sauce has thickened and reduced.

2 Add the mustard and fresh coriander/cilantro to the pan and stir to combine, then take the pan off the heat, spoon the curry into serving bowls and serve hot, with your choice of rice or flatbreads alongside.

Beetroot and Back-of-the-Fridge Curry

With its unique combination of sweet and earthy flavours, beetroot/beet is one of my favourite vegetables. The powerful aromatic spicing in this dish makes it a really good way to use up those vegetables at the back of your fridge that are going slightly soft and gnarled and look like they would put up with anything to save them from the compost. Yup, we are all headed there.

SERVES 4

250g/9oz new potatoes, quartered

4 tbsp vegetable oil

1 tsp panch phoron

500g/1lb 2oz cooked beetroot/beets, cut into 1½cm/5/8in pieces

¼ tsp ground turmeric

¼ tsp chilli powder

½ tsp salt

100g/3½oz greens (whatever you have that needs using up in the fridge), chopped

1 heaped tsp English mustard

½ tsp sugar

squeeze of lemon juice

cooked rice or flatbreads, to serve

1 Put the potatoes in a large pan, cover with salted water, place over a high heat and bring to a boil. Once the water is boiling, reduce the heat to a lively simmer and cook for 10 minutes, until the potatoes are tender. Drain through a colander and set aside.

2 Heat the oil in a separate pan over a medium heat, then add the panch phoron and cook, stirring, until the spice is fragrant and begins to fizz. Add the beetroot/beet chunks and cooked new potatoes and stir to combine with the oil and spice, then add the ground turmeric, chilli powder and salt, and stir again. Cover the pan with a lid and leave to cook for 8 minutes, stirring occasionally.

3 Stir the chopped greens through the mixture, then return the lid to the pan and leave to cook for another 3 minutes, until the greens are tender. Once everything is cooked through, remove the lid from the pan and stir through the mustard, sugar and 2 tablespoons of water. Squeeze over lemon juice to taste, then serve the curry with your choice of rice or flatbreads alongside.

Aubergine and Shallot Curry

Aubergines/eggplants love oil. They come alive with flavour and texture when they can drink as much as you will give them and they exchange their astringency for sweet, fleshy velvet. Make sure the aubergine is fried until soft and translucent in this dish, which will take some time, but is still an easy half-hour cook. Paired with the silky aubergine, ribbons of sweet shallot weave heady magic into this timeless combination of ingredients.

SERVES 4

125ml/4fl oz/½ cup vegetable oil
1 tsp fenugreek seeds
1 clove garlic, crushed
6 round shallots halved, and finely sliced
2 large aubergines/eggplants, cut into
   1.5 cm/⅝ in pieces

½ tsp ground turmeric
¼ tsp chilli powder
1 tsp ground coriander
1 tsp salt
small handful coriander/cilantro,
   stalks and leaves roughly chopped

1 Heat the oil in a large pan over a medium heat, then add the fenugreek seeds and fry for a few seconds until fragrant and just turning golden (be careful not to burn them, as this imparts a bitter flavour). Add the garlic and stir to combine with the fenugreek, then add the shallots and cook, stirring occasionally, for 5 minutes, until soft and translucent.

2 Add the aubergine/eggplant pieces to the pan and cook until the exposed flesh is a light golden colour. Reduce the heat to low, then add the ground turmeric, chilli powder, ground coriander and salt. Stir to combine the aubergines and shallots with the spices, then cover the pan with a lid and leave to cook, stirring occasionally, for 12–15 minutes, until the aubergines are tender. Stir through the fresh chopped coriander/cilantro and serve hot.

Green Bean and Mango Dahl

With this dish, the bigger and greener the mango, the better. When mangoes are unripe or underripe, they impart a fresher fragrance than their softer, sweeter counterparts. This dahl is all about that fresh fragrance, and is further enhanced by the elegance of the green beans combined with the young fruit.

SERVES 4

250g/9oz/1½ cups red lentils

1 large, green mango, peeled, stoned and cut into 1½cm/⅝ in pieces

200g/7oz canned chopped tomatoes

½ tsp ground turmeric

3 tbsp vegetable oil

1 tsp cumin seeds

1 fat green chilli, sliced

100g/3½oz runner or green beans, cut into quarters

1 tsp sugar

1½ tsp salt

juice of ½ lemon

small bunch coriander/cilantro, roughly chopped

1 Put the lentils, mango, chopped tomatoes, ground turmeric and 1l/1¾ pints/generous 4 cups of boiling water in a large pan over a medium heat. Bring to the boil, then reduce the heat to a simmer, cover the pan with a lid and leave to cook for 15 minutes, until the lentils are soft.

2 When the lentils are almost cooked, heat the oil in a non-stick frying pan/skillet over a medium heat, then add the cumin seeds and fry for a few seconds, until fragrant and dark golden brown. Add the sliced chilli to the pan and fry, stirring continuously, for 10 seconds, then add the runner or green beans and cook, still stirring, for 2 minutes. Tip the contents of the frying pan into the pan with the lentils and stir to combine.

3 Add the sugar, salt and lemon juice to the pan and stir to combine, then spoon the dahl into serving dishes and garnish with fresh chopped coriander/cilantro before serving.

Crunchy Poppy Seed Potatoes

It is important to seek out white poppy seeds for this recipe, which are a common fixture of Indian cuisine and milder in flavour than the black kind, often found in Eastern European desserts. Frying the nigella and poppy seeds and dressing potatoes with them gives the finished dish a lovely nutty flavour and pleasing crunch that is hard to beat.

SERVES 4

500g/1lb 2oz new potatoes, quartered
4 tbsp vegetable oil
1 tsp nigella seeds
2 tbsp white poppy seeds
2 long green chillies, sliced
¼ tsp salt
100g/3½oz spinach, shredded
cooked rice or flatbreads, to serve

1 Put the potatoes in a large pan, cover with cold, salted water, then place over a high heat and bring to a boil. Once boiling, reduce the heat to a simmer and cook for 8–10 minutes, until just tender. Drain through a colander and set aside.

2 When the potatoes are cooked, heat the oil in a separate pan over a medium heat. Add the nigella seeds and fry for a few seconds until they begin to pop, then add the poppy seeds and cook for a further few seconds, until they turn brown. Add the sliced chillies to the pan along with the potatoes and stir to combine. Season with the salt, then leave to cook for 8–10 minutes, stirring occasionally, until the potatoes are crisp and golden.

3 Add the spinach to the pan and stir to combine with the potatoes, until wilted. Remove the pan from the heat and spoon the potatoes into serving bowls. Serve hot with rice or flatbreads alongside, if you like.

Tangy Roasted Cauliflower

This is a wonderful way to cook cauliflower – tangy and lip smacking! You can get green mango powder in any Asian grocer where it is often sold as *amchoor*. It is what Indians use to bring sharpness to their dishes. If you can't get hold of it, blend the flesh of an underripe mango with a little lemon juice and use that instead. Remember, don't leave the cauliflower florets too big as they take longer to cook.

SERVES 4

1 large cauliflower, leaves removed and reserved, head cut into small florets
2 tbsp ground coriander
1 tbsp amchoor

1 tbsp salt
1 clove garlic, crushed
150ml/5fl oz/generous ½ cup vegetable oil

1 Preheat the oven to 200°C/400°F/gas mark 6 and line a baking sheet with foil.

2 Put the cauliflower leaves and florets in a large bowl and add the ground coriander, amchoor, salt, garlic and oil. Give everything a toss to combine the cauliflower with the oil and spices, then tip the mixture onto the prepared baking sheet, spreading everything out in an even layer. Transfer to the oven and bake for 15–20 minutes, until the cauliflower is golden and the leaves are crisp. Serve hot.

Rice Krispie Bhel Puri

Bhel Puri is a common street-food snack in India that is made with fried chickpea/garbanzo beans threads, puffed rice and roasted peanuts, and dressed with all that is hot and sharp. When my parents first came to the UK, they missed this mid-morning snack dreadfully, so invented this version using a well-known breakfast cereal. It's as ludicrous a secret pleasure as any Indian family could have.

SERVES 4

100g/3½oz/4 cups crisped rice cereal
   (such as Rice Krispies)
3 tbsp mustard oil
1 handful roasted peanuts
2 mild green chillies, finely chopped

1 red onion, finely chopped
1 small bunch coriander/cilantro,
   leaves and stalks finely chopped
1 tsp chaat masala
squeeze of lemon juice

1 Place a small frying pan/skillet over a low heat and add the crisped rice cereal. Warm the cereal for 3 minutes, tossing in the pan to prevent it from catching, then transfer to a large bowl. Add the rest of the ingredients and stir until everything is well combined. Serve immediately, while the cereal is still warm and crisp.

Ginger Beer, Onion and Broccoli Bhajis

Everyone needs a bhaji recipe up their sleeve. These golden, nutty offerings are what we serve to welcome guests, and can be made with a combination of onions and whatever other vegetables you have to hand, so be brave and give them a go. I love to use the fieriest ginger beer I can find, as it gives the batter a wonderfully tangy flavour.

SERVES 4

260g/9½oz/generous 2 cups gram/
   chickpea flour
¼ tsp bicarbonate of soda/baking soda
1 tsp ajwain seeds
1 tsp nigella seeds
1 tbsp white poppy seeds
300ml/10fl oz/1¼ cups ginger beer
   (the fierier the better)
1½ tsp salt
juice of 1 lemon

1 tsp ground coriander
1 tsp ground cumin
¼ tsp chilli powder
1 onion, roughly chopped
2 cloves garlic, crushed
150g/5½oz broccoli, stems and florets
   cut into bite-sized pieces
2 tbsp chopped fresh coriander/cilantro
vegetable oil, for frying
chutney or raita, to serve

1 Pour 5cm/2in of vegetable oil into the base of a wok or deep frying pan/skillet. Place over a medium heat until the oil has reached 180°C/350°F, gas mark 4, making sure it does not overheat. Alternatively, fill a deep-fat fryer with oil according to manufacturers' instructions and preheat to 180°C/350°F.

2 While the oil is heating, put the flour, bicarbonate of soda/baking soda, ajwain, nigella and poppy seeds into a large bowl and stir to combine. Pour in the ginger beer and whisk the mixture to a smooth batter, the consistency of single/pouring cream. Add the salt, lemon juice, ground coriander, ground cumin and chilli powder and whisk again to combine.

3 Add the onion, garlic, broccoli and fresh coriander to the bowl and stir to coat in everything in the batter.

4 Once the oil is at temperature, carefully drop tablespoons of the bhaji mixture into the oil in batches and cook for 2 minutes, until golden, then turn and cook on the other side for 2 minutes more. Remove from the pan with a slotted spoon and leave to drain on kitchen paper whilst you cook the rest of the bhajis.

5 Serve the bhajis hot with chutney or raita alongside, for dipping.

Indian French Toast

There are certain ingredients that Indians used to pimp western staples and they are ALL in this dish. It was inevitable that the billowy, comforting, any-time-of-day willingness of French toast would fall under the sights of my mother's artillery of spices, and this is the result. I know that this is spicy and oniony, but I still drizzle over a little maple syrup … don't judge me.

SERVES 4

8 eggs

100ml/3½fl oz/scant ½ cup whole or semi-skimmed milk

½ small onion, very finely chopped

2 mild green chillies, very finely chopped

1 tbsp ground coriander

½ tsp ground cumin

3 tbsp finely chopped fresh coriander/cilantro

½ tsp salt

freshly ground black pepper

4 tsp unsalted butter

4 tsp vegetable oil

8 slices bread

maple syrup, for drizzling (optional)

1 Crack the eggs into a large bowl, then add the milk, onion, finely chopped chillies, ground coriander, ground cumin, fresh coriander/cilantro, salt and a generous grinding of black pepper. Beat with a fork until everything is well combined, then set aside.

2 Heat 1 teaspoon each of the butter and oil in a large non-stick pan over a medium heat.

3 While the butter is melting, dip one slice of the bread into the egg mixture until nicely soaked and crusted with the onion, herbs and spices. Lay the coated bread in the hot pan and cook for 2 minutes, then flip and cook on the other side for another 2 minutes, until crisp and golden. Remove from the pan, set aside and keep warm while you repeat the process with the remaining oil, butter and bread. Serve hot, drizzled with a little maple syrup, if you like.

Date-Spiced Paneer

Paneer is now available from most supermarkets, and although to the uninitiated it can seem hard and unyielding, when simmered in fragrant sauce it quickly becomes soft and delicious. I love the fruity caramel note that dates add to this dish – if you can't get hold of date molasses, don't worry, simply add a teaspoon of muscovado sugar with the chopped dates and the results will still be spectacular.

SERVES 4

5 tbsp vegetable oil

600g/1lb 5oz paneer, cut into
  long fingers

1 onion, halved and finely sliced

1 cube frozen crushed garlic
  or 3 garlic cloves, crushed

1 cube frozen crushed ginger
  or 2 thumb-sized pieces fresh
  ginger, peeled and grated

100g/3½oz dried dates, finely chopped

½ tsp ground cinnamon

½ tsp ground turmeric

½ tsp chilli flakes

½ tsp ground cumin

3 tbsp date molasses

1 tsp salt

50g/1¾oz/generous ½ cup flaked/
  slivered almonds

1 Heat 2 tablespoons of the oil in a large frying pan/skillet over a medium heat, then add the paneer and cook, turning occasionally, for around 5 minutes, until golden on all sides. Set aside.

2 Meanwhile, heat the remaining 2 tablespoons of oil in a separate frying pan, then add the onion, garlic and ginger and cook for 8 minutes, stirring occasionally, until golden brown. Add the chopped dates, ground cinnamon, ground turmeric, chilli flakes, ground cumin, date molasses, salt and 250ml/9fl oz/generous 1 cup of boiling water to the pan and stir to combine. Bring the mixture to the boil, then reduce to a simmer and leave to cook for 5–8 minutes, until thick and glossy.

3 Add the paneer to the pan with the sauce and stir to coat, being careful not to break the fingers of paneer as you do. Leave to simmer for 5 minutes.

4 Meanwhile, return the pan that you cooked the paneer in to the heat and add the flaked almonds. Cook, stirring occasionally, until golden brown, then add the almonds into the pan with the paneer and stir briefly to combine. Serve hot.

144

Street-Hawker Sweetcorn

Nothing speaks of a late-night street market in the East more than the golden flickering embers of a sweetcorn hawker's stall. The delicious combination of sharp and heat make these far more than a side show – they are the very reason that many venture out into the streets at all. These are great cooked under the grill/broiler or on the barbecue. For extra theatre, I like to ask my guests to dress their own pieces of corn before cooking.

SERVES 4
2 tbsp olive oil
½ tsp salt
½ tsp chilli powder
1 tsp ground cumin
1 lime, halved
4 corn on the cob

1 Preheat the grill/broiler to high and line a grill pan with foil, or prepare a barbecue/grill for cooking.

2 Put the oil, salt, chilli powder and ground cumin in a bowl and stir to combine. Dip the cut sides of the lime halves into the oil-and-spice mixture, then rub all over the pieces of corn. Re-dipping as necessary, until the corn is well coated.

3 Put the corn onto the prepared grill pan and under the grill, or place directly onto the barbecue and cook for 10–15 minutes, turning regularly and basting with any remaining spiced oil, until lightly charred and golden all over. Serve hot.

147

Melon and Feta Salad

It is very common in India to eat melon with a little bit of salt on the side to bring out the sweetness and make it all the more refreshing. The lovely salty tang of feta cheese does the same in this dish. It may sound like an unlikely combination, but it is very special, and I urge you to give it a try.

SERVES 4
¼ watermelon (approx. 1kg/2lb 4oz), peeled and cut into bite-sized pieces
1 honeydew melon, peeled, deseeded and cut into bite-sized pieces
200g/7oz feta cheese, cut into 1cm/ ½in pieces

juice of 1 lime
1 tbsp runny honey
¼ tsp ground cumin
½ tsp chaat masala or salt
1 small bunch mint, leaves picked and finely chopped

1 Put both types of melon and the feta cheese in a large bowl and toss together to combine, then tip out onto a serving platter. Drizzle the lime juice over the melon and cheese, followed by the honey. Using a sieve/strainer, dust the salad with the ground cumin and chaat masala or salt, then scatter over the chopped fresh mint. Serve.

Indian Scrambled Eggs

Indians love their scrambled egg cooked until very dry. We fry it until all the moisture has evaporated and the spices comes to the fore. You can, of course, opt for a softer, more yielding texture, here, though I encourage you to try it the traditional way at least once. This is gorgeous on fried bread or toast and yes, ketchup is very much a legitimate accompaniment, although if you can get hold of garlic and chilli sauce, so much the better.

SERVES 4

4 tbsp vegetable oil

1 small onion, finely chopped

1 cube frozen crushed garlic
or 3 garlic cloves, crushed

1 cube frozen crushed ginger
or 1 thumb-sized pieces fresh
ginger, peeled and grated

¼ cauliflower (approx. 200g/7oz),
grated

½ tsp ground turmeric

½ tbsp ground coriander

8 eggs

½ tsp salt

½ tsp freshly ground black pepper

1 tomato, finely chopped, to garnish

2 tbsp finely chopped fresh coriander/
cilantro, to garnish

toast or fried bread and ketchup or chilli
sauce, to serve

1 Heat the oil in a large, non-stick frying pan/skillet over a medium heat, then add the onion, garlic and ginger and cook, stirring occasionally, for about 5 minutes, until the onion is soft and translucent. Add the cauliflower, ground turmeric and ground coriander and cook, stirring occasionally, for 2 minutes.

2 Crack the eggs into a large jug, add the salt and pepper, and beat with a fork to combine. Reduce the heat under the pan to low, then tip in the eggs and cook, stirring continuously, until scrambled to your liking. (Traditionally, this would be served with the eggs cooked until dry and granular, but I know that western palates often prefer a softer, more pillowy texture.)

3 Divide the eggs between serving plates and garnish with the tomatoes and fresh coriander/cilantro. Serve hot, with toast or fried bread and ketchup or chilli sauce.

Courgette and Spiced Peanut Salad

Courgettes/zucchini go a long way when shaved into ribbons in a salad and are great at absorbing all the flavour that surrounds them. It's better to use roasted peanuts in this dish to balance the sharpness of the dressing and add a much-needed crunch. If you have an intolerance to nuts, I have been known to add dry-roasted chickpeas/garbanzo beans instead.

SERVES 4

2 courgettes/zucchini

150g/5½oz cherry tomatoes, halved

3 tbsp chopped fresh mint leaves,
    to garnish

100g/3½oz/¾ cup roasted peanuts,
    to garnish

For the dressing:

juice of 2 limes

¼ tsp chilli powder

1 tsp brown sugar

½ clove garlic, crushed

3 tbsp fish sauce

2 tbsp sesame oil

1 Using a ribbon peeler, slice the courgettes/zucchini into fine ribbons and place in a large serving bowl. Add the cherry tomatoes to the bowl and set aside while you prepare the dressing.

2 To make the dressing, combine all the ingredients in a small jug or bowl and whisk to incorporate. Pour the dressing over the courgettes and tomatoes and toss gently to combine, then garnish the salad with the fresh chopped mint and roasted peanuts. Serve immediately.

Egg and Watercress Curry

Egg curry is very popular in India and every family has their own recipe. I love to give mine a real wake-up call with the addition of fiery English mustard and peppery watercress. The resulting combination of flavours performs a lively dance across your tongue that I can't get enough of.

SERVES 4

8 eggs
4 tbsp vegetable oil
1 tsp cumin seeds
2 onions, roughly chopped
2 cubes frozen crushed garlic
    or 6 garlic cloves, crushed
2 cubes frozen crushed ginger
    or 2 thumb-sized pieces fresh
    ginger, peeled and grated

400g/14oz canned chopped tomatoes
1 tsp ground turmeric
2 tbsp garam masala
1 fat green chilli, sliced
1½ tsp salt
2 tsp sugar
85g/3oz watercress, finely chopped
2 tbsp English mustard
cooked rice, to serve

1 Bring a large pan of water to the boil over a high heat, then reduce the heat to a lively simmer. Carefully add the eggs to the pan and leave to boil for 8 minutes, then drain through a colander and run under cold water until cool enough to peel.

2 While the eggs are boiling, heat 2 tablespoons of the oil in a large, non-stick frying pan/skillet over a medium heat, then add the cumin seeds and fry for a few seconds until fragrant and dark golden brown. Add the onions, garlic and ginger to the pan and cook for 2 minutes, stirring continuously, until soft. Add the chopped tomatoes, ground turmeric and garam masala to the pan and stir to combine, then leave to cook, stirring occasionally, for 10 minutes, until the sauce has thickened and darkened slightly.

3 While the sauce is cooking, peel the eggs. Heat the remaining 2 tablespoons of oil in a separate frying pan/skillet over medium heat, then add the eggs and cook, moving them around in the pan, for 2–3 minutes, until golden on all sides.

4 Add the sliced chilli to the sauce and stir to combine, then carefully stir through the fried, hard-boiled eggs along with the salt, sugar, watercress, mustard and a little water, if you feel the sauce is too thick. Cook for 3–4 minutes to let everything meld together, then remove from the heat, spoon the curry into serving bowls and serve with rice alongside.

5
MA, LOOK AWAY!

This chapter is all about bringing life to all that is asleep and hard as nails in your pantry or storecupboard. You'll find a lot of pasta and noodle dishes here, but I have not included anything that requires you to flex your culinary muscles too much. These are the dishes for the days when life is hectic and you need something tasty and sustaining on the table in a flash, without the need for forward planning or mastery of technique.

Despite the ease with which recipes can be thrown together, these are real crowd-pleasers, especially among the younger members of the household who, in general, I have found to have an insatiable appetite for comforting pasta and slippery noodles. I am grateful to Italy and Korea for this, which, after India, are my other culinary homelands.

This handful of recipes is not the food you might expect from a Mowgli book, but it is the food that adorns the stove-top in my kitchen, the root of all things Mowgli, on a regular basis, and as such, I couldn't put together a collection of home-cooking recipes without it. Ma, look away!

Six-Minute Tomato Pasta

This is the simplest and most comforting of dishes, and we have it at least twice a week at home. Children and adults alike will love it, and once you've mastered it, you'll never feel the urge to reach for a jar of pre-made pasta sauce again.

SERVES 4

300g/10½oz dried spaghetti
2 tbsp olive oil
2 tsp garlic purée
400g/14oz canned chopped tomatoes
1 tsp ground turmeric

2 tsp brown sugar
2 sprigs fresh thyme, leaves picked
2 ham stock cubes (veg also work well)
1 tbsp roughly chopped fresh parsley,
   to garnish
sea salt and freshly ground black pepper

1 Bring a large pan of salted water to the boil over a high heat. Add the spaghetti and cook for 6–8 minutes, according to packet instructions, until *al dente*.

2 Meanwhile, heat the oil in a large pan over a medium heat, then add the garlic purée and cook, stirring, for 1 minute, until fragrant but not coloured. Add the chopped tomatoes to the pan, then rinse the tomato can with a splash of water and add that to the pan also. Add the ground turmeric, sugar and thyme, and crumble in the stock cubes, then season with black pepper and stir to combine. Bring the sauce to the boil, then reduce to a simmer and leave to cook for 5 minutes, until the oil rises to the surface of and pools around the edges of the pan.

3 Drain the spaghetti, then tip it into the pan with the sauce, bringing a ladleful of the pasta water along with it. Stir the spaghetti into the sauce until well coated, then divide the mixture between serving plates and garnish with the parsley. Serve hot.

Lemon Chicken Pasta

I must confess that the spark of an idea for this recipe started in a department-store café, when I tasted something similar, loved it and decided to try and recreate it at home. It soon became a family staple and it's one of the few dishes that my daughters actively sought out the recipe for. The sharp tang of the lemon combined with the nursery comfort of the pasta is reminiscent of the zingy crêpes that are so beloved in my household. It sounds odd, I know, but do give it a try – it's a dish that I hold very close to my heart.

SERVES 4

300g/10½oz dried spaghetti
2 tbsp vegetable oil
1 cube frozen crushed garlic
    or 3 garlic cloves, crushed
4 skinless, boneless chicken breasts,
    cut into bite-sized pieces
½ tsp ground turmeric

2 tbsp sugar
sea salt and freshly ground black pepper
2 chicken stock cubes, crumbled
juice of 1 lemon
150ml/5fl oz/generous ½ cup
    crème fraîche
2 tbsp snipped chives

162

1 Bring a large pan of salted water to the boil over a high heat. Add the spaghetti and cook for 10–12 minutes, according to packet instructions, until tender.

2 Heat the oil in a large pan over a medium heat, then add the garlic and cook, stirring continuously, for 2 minutes, until softened but not coloured. Increase the heat to high, then add the chicken and continue to cook, stirring, until sealed on all sides. Once the chicken has sealed and has started to release liquid, add the ground turmeric and sugar, season generously with salt and pepper and crumble over the chicken stock cubes. Stir to combine and continue to cook, stirring occasionally, for 5 minutes, until the chicken is cooked through.

3 Drain the pasta through a colander, adding a ladleful of the pasta water to the pan with the chicken as you do so. Add the lemon juice and crème fraîche to the pan and stir to combine. Divide the spaghetti between serving plates and spoon the chicken and sauce over the top. Sprinkle with chives and serve immediately.

Godfather Pasta

I love films that take you into people's kitchens and show you how they eat. The scene in *The Godfather* where Pete Clemenza teaches Michael Corleone how to cook his meatball pasta has always held a grip on my heart, so much so that I recreated his recipe by playing the film over and over whilst I cooked along at the hob. I have to say the result was magnificent. So here it is for you because, as Clemenza says, "You never know, you might have to cook for 20 guys someday".

SERVES 4

2 tbsp olive oil

1 cube frozen crushed garlic
   or 3 garlic cloves, crushed

3 tbsp tomato purée

400g/14oz canned chopped tomatoes

175ml/6fl oz/¾ cup red wine

2 tbsp sugar

300g/10½oz dried spaghetti

4 pork and fennel sausages,
   cut into 2½cm/1in pieces

350g/12oz pack ready-made
   beef meatballs

1 Heat the oil in a large pan over a medium heat, then add the garlic and cook, stirring continuously, for 2 minutes, until softened but not coloured. Add the tomato purée, chopped tomatoes, red wine and sugar to the pan and stir to combine. Bring the mixture to the boil, then reduce to a simmer and cook for around 5 minutes, until the oil rises to the surface and pools around the outside edge of the sauce.

2 Meanwhile, bring a large pan of salted water to the boil, add the spaghetti and cook for 10–12 minutes, according to packet instructions, until tender.

3 Add the sausages and meatballs to the pan with the sauce and stir to combine, then leave to cook for 12 minutes, until the meat is cooked through and the sauce is thickened and reduced.

4 Drain the spaghetti, adding a ladleful of the pasta water to the pan with the sauce, then divide the spaghetti between the serving bowls and spoon the sauce, meatballs and sausages over the top. Serve hot.

Korean Noodles

In my quest to explore the world's cuisines, I have been lucky enough to travel to Korea to learn to cook their food. Fresh, vibrant and punchy, I think it's one of my favourite cuisines in the world. This is my super-simple take on a classic Korean noodle dish, called *Japchae*, and is simple, healthy and quick to throw together for a delicious supper. Sweet potato noodles are worth the effort of hunting out, as they have a unique bounce and elasticity that makes them really fun to eat. They should be available in any Asian grocers, but if you can't find them, any other glass or rice noodles would do in a pinch.

SERVES 4

1 tbsp vegetable oil

1 onion, halved and finely sliced

1 carrot, peeled and cut into matchsticks

3 cubes frozen crushed garlic
  or 9 garlic cloves, crushed

300g/10½oz sweet potato
  vermicelli noodles

1 red pepper, deseeded and sliced

1 yellow pepper, deseeded and sliced

5 chestnut/cremini mushrooms, sliced

50g/1¾oz green beans, cut into thirds

6 tbsp light soy sauce

2 tbsp brown sugar

2 tbsp sesame oil

2 tbsp roughly chopped fresh coriander/
  cilantro

1 Heat the oil over a medium heat in a large, non-stick frying pan/skillet or wok, then add the onion, carrot and garlic and cook, stirring continuously, for 4–5 minutes, until soft.

2 Meanwhile, put the vermicelli noodles in a bowl and pour over boiling water to cover, then set aside for a few minutes to soften.

3 Increase the heat under the frying pan/skillet or wok to high, then add the sliced peppers, mushrooms and green beans and continue to cook, stirring or tossing the pan, for 2 minutes.

4 Drain the noodles and add them to the pan with the vegetables, then add the soy sauce, brown sugar and sesame oil and toss or stir the pan to make sure everything is well coated. Remove the pan from the heat and divide the mixture between 4 serving bowls, then scatter over the fresh coriander/cilantro and serve hot.

Oozy Tuna and Apple Pasta Bake

I love dishes that wake up those ingredients hibernating at the back of your storecupboard. This recipe breathes new life into canned tuna, canned tomatoes and dry pasta, making it is a great option when the fridge is bare. The apple is the real game changer here and it adds an interesting twist and a lovely bite to this superb traybake.

SERVES 4

350g/12oz dried spaghetti
   (or leftover cooked spaghetti)
3 tbsp olive oil
1 cube frozen crushed garlic
   or 3 garlic cloves, crushed
800g/1lb 12oz canned chopped
   tomatoes
1 tsp ground turmeric
½ tsp sugar
sea salt and freshly ground black pepper
190g/6½oz canned tuna, drained
1 tbsp capers
2 apples, grated
1 tbsp tomato purée
150g/5½oz/generous 1½ cups grated
   Cheddar or Gloucester cheese

1 Preheat the oven to 200°C/400°F/gas mark 6.

2 If using uncooked spaghetti, bring a large pan of salted water to the boil over a high heat. Add the spaghetti and cook for 6–8 minutes, according to packet instructions, until *al dente*.

3 Meanwhile, heat the oil in a large pan over a medium heat, then add the garlic and cook, stirring continuously, for 2 minutes, until fragrant but not coloured. Add the chopped tomatoes, ground turmeric, sugar and season with salt and pepper, then stir to combine. Bring the mixture to the boil, then reduce to a simmer. Flake the drained tuna into the pan and add the capers, grated apples and tomato purée. Leave to cook, stirring occasionally for 5 minutes.

4 Once the spaghetti is cooked, drain it through a colander and use scissors to snip it into bite-size lengths. Add the snipped spaghetti to the pan with the sauce and stir to combine until the pasta is well coated. Add half of the grated cheese to the pan and stir to combine, then tip the mixture into a baking dish in an even layer. Scatter over the remaining grated cheese, then transfer to the oven to bake for 15 minutes, until the top is crisp and golden and the sauce is bubbling. Spoon the pasta bake into serving bowls and serve hot.

6

DESSERTS
AND DRINKS

It's very rare that I would actually cook any kind of dessert on a day-to-day basis. Instead, I tend to opt for a sweeter main course on days where my sugar cravings need sating. I was never raised to bake at my grandmother's elbow, and cakes and cookies do not form part of my culinary DNA.

The desserts I do make are, by and large, cooked in a pan on the stove-top and are comforting and sweetly spoonable when ready. The Corner-Shop Brownies (p.176) in this chapter are a notable exception. My children were born and raised entirely in the west and here they discovered the alchemy of weighing, measuring and melting to create the desserts of their dreams.

The other dishes in this collection of sweet treats are those that have captured my heart from street-food markets and neighbourhood cafés across the world. And no meal would be complete without a fragrant, steaming cup of tea or coffee at the finish, so I have added those as well.

School-Skive Semolina Cake

As a child, whenever I was unwell and had to stay home from school, my mother would always reach into her apothecary drawers and bring out the semolina. It was warming, nutty and completely comforting, and this cake is an elegant version of all of those things. I added the gold leaf and the green cardamon to give it a dinner-party finesse, but at its heart, semolina will always be plain comfort to me.

SERVES 15

300ml/10fl oz/1¼ cups whole milk
200g/7oz/1 cup light muscovado sugar
50g/1¾oz ghee
1 green cardamom pod
225g/8oz/1⅓ cups fine semolina
¼ tsp salt

2 tbsp plain/all-purpose flour, sifted
1½ tsp baking powder
¼ tsp bicarbonate of soda/baking soda
125g/4½oz/scant ½ cup plain yoghurt
15 blanched whole almonds
edible gold leaf, to decorate (optional)

1 Preheat the oven to 180°C/350°F/gas mark 4 and grease and line a 28 x 20cm/11 x 8in baking tin with baking parchment.

2 Put the milk and sugar in a small pan and place over a gentle heat, stirring until the sugar dissolves. Set aside.

3 In a separate large pan, melt the ghee over a low heat. Crush the cardamom pod in a pestle and mortar to release the seeds, then discard the outer husk and crush the seeds gently. Add the lightly crushed cardamom seeds to the pan with the melted ghee and cook gently for 1 minute to allow the flavours to infuse.

4 With the pan still on the heat, add the semolina and salt to the ghee and sift in the flour, baking powder and bicarbonate of soda/baking soda. Stirring continuously, slowly pour the warmed milk mixture into the pan and continue to cook, stirring, until the semolina has absorbed the milk and you have smooth-batter consistency.

5 Remove the pan from the heat and fold the yoghurt through the mixture, then pour the batter into the prepared tin and spread out in an even layer. Arrange the almonds over the top of the cake batter, then transfer to the preheated oven and bake for 20 minutes, until firm, well risen and golden.

6 Leave the cake to cool for 10 minutes in the tin, then tip out onto a cooling rack and leave to cool to room temperature. Once cooled, decorate the surface of the cake with squares of gold leaf, if using, and slice into squares to serve.

174

Corner-Shop Brownies

As young girls, whenever my daughters had pocket money they would nip to the corner shop and buy whatever was chocolatey, knobbly and oozy. They would then melt the loot together and take great pride in reforming the primordial ooze into sweet and squidgy brownies, a ritual that got refined and perfected over the years to culminate in this recipe

SERVES 8-10

150g/5½oz milk chocolate,
  broken into squares
150g/5½oz unsalted butter, cubed
2 eggs
70g/2½oz/scant ½ cup caster/
  superfine sugar
70g/2½oz/scant ½ cup soft
  brown sugar

1 tbsp cocoa powder
100g/3½oz/¾ cup plain/all-purpose
  flour
sea salt
40g/1½oz tube Rolos
50g/1¾oz pack Maltesers
25g/1oz mini marshmallows

1 Preheat the oven to 200°C/400°F/gas mark 6 and grease a square 20 cm/8in cake pan or brownie tin with butter and line with baking parchment.

2 Put the chocolate and butter in a heatproof bowl and either set over a pan of simmering water or heat in short bursts in the microwave, until melted.

3 Crack the eggs into a separate bowl and add both types of sugar, then, using an electric whisk, beat together until thickened and doubled in volume. Pour the butter-and-chocolate mixture into the bowl with the eggs and sugar and gently fold in to combine. Sift the cocoa powder, flour and a pinch of salt into the bowl and gently fold into the wet ingredients, then fold through half of the Rolos, Maltesers and marshmallows.

4 Pour the mixture into the prepared tin and level out the surface with a spatula, then scatter over the remaining Rolos, Maltesers and marshmallows. Transfer the tin to the oven and bake the brownies for 15–20 minutes, until crisp at the edges but still with a slight wobble in the centre. Remove the tin from the oven and set aside to cool for 10 minutes, then use the baking parchment to carefully lift out the brownies, slice into squares and serve.

Aunty Geeta's String Pudding

When Aunty Geeta would come and visit, we would frisk her at the door for two things: the first was her prawn/shrimp curry and the other was this fantastic string pudding. It's basically a really homely rice pudding, but uses very fine vermicelli instead of the rice, making it stringy and fun and delicious.

SERVES 4

2 tbsp ghee
120g/4½oz fine vermicelli noodles
640ml/22fl oz/generous 2½ cups
   full-fat milk

100g/3½oz/½ cup caster/superfine
   sugar
2 green cardamom pods, seeds crushed
½ tsp saffron threads
3 tbsp flaked almonds

1 Melt the ghee in a large pan over a medium heat. Once the ghee has melted, add the dried vermicelli noodles to the pan and fry for around 2 minutes, until golden brown and well coated in the ghee.

2 Reduce the heat to low, then pour the milk into the pan and heat until it reaches a gentle simmer. Add the sugar and stir the mixture until the sugar has dissolved, then add the cardamom seeds and saffron threads and stir again to combine. Cook the mixture for 5–6 minutes, until the milk has thickened and the noodles are tender.

3 Remove the pan from the heat and stir through the flaked almonds. Spoon the pudding into serving bowls and serve hot.

DESSERTS AND DRINKS

Mango and Mint Fool

You should be able to find Alphonso or Kesar mango pulp in any Asian grocers, but you could use tinned mango slices or even fresh mango without any issues here. Mint and mango work wonderfully together, and this simple dessert is sweet, creamy and refreshing. The perfect way to end a meal.

SERVES 4

425g/15oz canned Alphonso mango pulp or tinned mango slices
juice and zest of 1 lime
175ml/6fl oz double/heavy cream

2 tsp caster/superfine sugar
3 tbsp Greek yoghurt
2 tbsp chopped fresh mint leaves
1 tbsp toasted coconut flakes

1 Put the mango pulp or slices and lime juice into the bowl of a food processor and process until smooth. Set aside.

2 Pour the double/heavy cream into a bowl and beat with an electric or handheld whisk until soft peaks form. Add the sugar, yoghurt and mint leaves to the bowl and fold through the cream, then add the mango purée and gently ripple it through the cream mixture.

3 Spoon the mixture into serving bowls or glasses and transfer to fridge to set for 15–20 minutes, or longer if you want to make this ahead. Garnish the fools with the lime zest and toasted coconut flakes before serving.

Coconut and Chia Seed Pots

I first came across these in Amsterdam about 25 years ago and remember thinking how very *avant-garde* they were. That was the beginning of the chia-seed revolution and since then they have become ever more ubiquitous. Though they have the slight whiff of the health-food shop on them, they are actually utterly delicious as well as being good for you – win, win! Though these are in the desserts section, these would be equally welcome at the breakfast table, or for a pick-me-up at any time of day. The setting time for these does push this recipe beyond the 30-minute mark, but the assembly is so speedy and they are so wonderful to make the evening before and have waiting in the fridge that I'll hope you'll forgive me for that.

SERVES 4

70g/2½oz chia seeds
400ml/14fl oz canned light coconut milk
3 tbsp runny honey
1 tsp vanilla extract
3 tbsp unsweetened desiccated coconut
1 tbsp toasted coconut flakes and
     a handful of raspberries, to garnish

1 Put the chia seeds, coconut milk, honey, vanilla extract and desiccated coconut in a bowl and stir to combine. Leave to stand for 10 minutes, stirring occasionally, then divide the mixture between 4 ramekins or serving glasses. Transfer to the fridge and leave for at least an hour or up till overnight, until set to a pudding-like consistency. Garnish the pots with toasted coconut flakes and fresh raspberries before serving.

Balsamic and Anise Fruit

This dessert is delicious and lightning quick to make, yet classic and classy enough to serve at the most grown-up of dinner parties. It can all be left until the last moment as you won't be away from the dinner table for long and, arms laden with this jewel-like platter of fruit, you will certainly be welcomed back with geat enthusiasm! I love the way the balsamic vinegar adds a sweet and dark bass note to the soft fruit. Serve with vanilla ice cream to soften the whole experience.

SERVES 4

115ml/3¾fl oz/scant ½ cup
   balsamic vinegar
2 tbsp soft brown sugar
1 star anise
2 medium ripe plums, stoned
   and cut into quarters

8 large strawberries, hulled
   and cut into quarters
4 figs, cut into quarters
vanilla ice cream, to serve

184

1 Put the balsamic vinegar, sugar and star anise in a small pan over a medium heat. Bring the mixture to the boil, then reduce to a simmer and leave to bubble away until the mixture has reduced by half.

2 Arrange the fruit on a serving platter or divide between bowls, then drizzle with the balsamic glaze. Serve with vanilla ice cream alongside.

Mango and Mint Lassi

In India, mango lassi can be found for sale on almost every street corner. In the heat of the day, it is the ultimate way to quench, refresh and rebalance. It's just as popular in my kitchen on the Wirral, though the weather is a lot more forgiving.

SERVES 4

425g/15oz canned Alphonso mango pulp or tinned mango slices

150ml/5fl oz/generous ½ cup plain yoghurt

150ml/5fl oz/generous ½ cup whole or semi-skimmed milk

juice of 1 lime

2 tbsp chopped fresh mint leaves

salt

1 Put the mango slices into the bowl of a food processor and process to a smooth pulp. Add the yoghurt, milk, lime juice and mint, then blend again until smooth. Divide the lassi between 4 glasses and serve immediately.

Traditional Masala Chai

Masala Chai is something that many Indians will have in the evening along with a couple of salted biscuits. It's usually a sweet milky tea with whole aromatic spices steeped in the liquor. I give you this version, but in truth you can add whatever spices you like, so feel free to play with the recipe and find the mix of spices that best soothes your soul at the end of a long, hard day.

SERVES 1

2 green cardamom pods
1 clove
thumb-sized piece fresh ginger, peeled
 and roughly chopped
1 tsp Assam tea
125ml/4 fl oz/½ cup whole milk
1 tbsp sugar, or to taste

1 Put the cardamom pods, clove and ginger in pestle and mortar and grind to a coarse paste. Set aside.

2 Bring 150ml/5fl oz/generous ½ cup of water to the boil in a small pan. Add the spice paste and leave to boil away for 2 minutes, the reduce the heat to low, add the Assam tea and leave to simmer for 2–5 minutes, depending on how strong you like your tea.

3 Add the milk and sugar to the pan and simmer for another 2 minutes, then taste the tea and add more sugar if necessary. Strain the chai through a fine-mesh strainer into a cup and serve hot.

Calcutta Cold Coffee

My ancestors come from Calcutta and my memories of days spent there in my youth are coloured with the glaring heat and intensity of the brutal summer sun. During these summers, cool relief could be found at the heaving stalls of street vendors who sold ice-cold, sweet coffee. I hope this recipe offers you the same relief.

SERVES 4
2 tbsp dark-roast instant coffee

400ml/14fl oz/scant 1¾ cups
   whole milk

6 tbsp sugar

1 green cardamom pod,
   seeds lightly crushed

1 black cardamom pod,
   seeds lightly crushed

4 cinnamon sticks, to serve

1 Put the coffee in a cup with just enough boiling water to dissolve it, then pour into a blender along with the milk, sugar and both types cardamom seeds. Blend the mixture to combine, then set aside for 10 minutes to allow the spices to infuse.

2 Fill 4 small glasses with crushed ice and add a cinnamon stick to each one, then pour the coffee into the glasses through a sieve/strainer. Enjoy!

Index

A

after-school pepper pot 84

almonds
 Aunty Geeta's string pudding 179
 cauliflower, sugar snap and almond
  curry 122
 chicken korma 45
 mango chicken curry 36

apples
 Mowgli coleslaw chicken bowl 57
 oozy tuna and apple pasta bake
  168

apricots: spiced lamb and apricot wraps
 68

aubergine and shallot curry 130

Aunty Geeta's string pudding 179

B

balsamic and anise fruit 184

beef
 godfather pasta 165
 rare spice-rubbed steak 71

beetroot and back-of-the-fridge curry
 128

Bengali fish curry 96

bhajis: ginger beer, onion and broccoli
 141

bhel puri, Rice Krispie 138

bread
 Indian fish finger sandwich 107
 Indian French toast 142
 keema toasties 72
 spiced lamb and apricot wraps 68

broccoli
 ginger beer, onion and broccoli
  bhajis 141
 minced pork and glass noodle broth 90
 prawn and broccoli curry 104
 yoghurt and coriander turkey with
  tenderstem broccoli 54

brownies: corner-shop 176

burgers: last-minute lamb 74

butter beans
 spiced butter bean curry 127
 super-simple tomato and nigella soup
  121

C

cabbage: Mowgli coleslaw chicken
 bowl 57

cakes and bakes
 corner-shop brownies 176
 school-skive semolina cake 174

Calcutta cold coffee 191

carrots
 keema toasties 72
 little sparrow pea soup 53
 Mowgli coleslaw chicken bowl 57

cashews
 chicken, coconut and pineapple curry
  39
 courgette and cashew curry 118

cauliflower
 cauliflower, sugar snap and almond
  curry 122

tangy roasted cauliflower 136

cheese
    date-spiced paneer 144
    melon and feta salad 148
    oozy tuna and apple pasta bake
        168

chia seeds: coconut and chia seed pots
    182

chicken 22, 32–3
    chicken and spinach curry 42
    chicken, coconut and pineapple curry
        39
    chicken dhansak 34
    chicken kofta curry 48
    chicken korma 45
    chicken papaya and green bean
        keema 60
    lemon chicken pasta 162
    mango chicken curry 36
    monsoon chicken and mushroom
        curry 58
    Mowgli coleslaw chicken bowl
        57
    paprika chicken 40
    quick angry tandoori 46
    sticky chicken thighs 51

chickpeas: spinach and chickpea curry
    124

chocolate: corner-shop brownies 176

chorizo
    after-school pepper pot 84
    little sparrow pea soup 53

coconut
    chicken, coconut and pineapple curry
        39
    chicken kofta curry 48
    coconut and chia seed pots 182

ginger and garlic mussels with lime
    leaves 101

spinach and chickpea curry 124

coffee: Calcutta cold coffee 191

coleslaw: Mowgli coleslaw chicken
    bowl 57

corner-shop brownies 176

courgettes
    courgette and cashew curry 118
    courgette and spiced peanut salad
        152

cream: mango and mint fool 180

crème fraîche
    chicken kofta curry 48
    chicken korma 45
    ginger beer pork 78
    lemon chicken pasta 162

D

dahl
    green bean and mango dahl 133
    million-dollar 116

date-spiced paneer 144

dhansak, chicken 34

drinks
    Calcutta cold coffee 191
    mango and mint lassi 186
    traditional masala chai 188

E

eggs
    curry house prawn and mushroom
        omelette 102
    eggs and watercress curry 155
    Indian French toast 142
    Indian scrambled eggs 151

F

feta: melon and feta salad 148
fish
   Bengali fish curry 96
   gin and tonic salmon 98
   Indian fish finger sandwich 107
   mango and coriander salmon 110
   oozy tuna and apple pasta bake
      168
   tamarind salmon curry 108
fool: mango and mint 180
French toast, Indian 142
fruit: balsamic and anise fruit 184

G

garlic 20
   ginger and garlic mussels with lime
      leaves 101
   wild garlic and lamb salad 89
gin and tonic salmon 98
ginger 20
   ginger and garlic mussels with lime
      leaves 101
ginger beer
   ginger beer, onion and broccoli
      bhajis 141
ginger beer pork 78
gingerbread lamb steaks 66
godfather pasta 165
green beans
   chicken papaya and green bean
      keema 60
   green bean and mango dahl 133
   minced pork and glass noodle broth
      90
greens: beetroot and back-of-the-fridge
   curry 128

I

Indian fish finger sandwich 107
Indian French toast 142
Indian scrambled eggs 151

K

keema
   chicken papaya and green bean 60
keema toasties 72
kofta: chicken kofta curry 48
Korean noodles 166
korma: chicken 45

L

lamb
   gingerbread lamb steaks 66
   keema toasties 72
   last-minute lamb burgers 74
   spiced lamb and apricot wraps 68
   spinach meatball curry 80
   sumac lamb steaks 83
   tandoori lamb chops 77
   ten-minute, late-night kebabs 86
   wild garlic and lamb salad 89
lassi: mango and mint 186
lemon chicken pasta 162
lentils
   chicken dhansak 34
   green bean and mango dahl 133
   million-dollar dahl 116
   little sparrow pea soup 53

M

mango
   green bean and mango dahl 133
   mango and coriander salmon 110

mango and mint fool 180

mango and mint lassi 186

mango chicken curry 36

masala chai 188

melon and feta salad 148

milk

Aunty Geeta's string pudding 179

Calcutta cold coffee 191

Indian French toast 142

school-skive semolina cake 174

traditional masala chai 188

million-dollar dahl 116

monsoon chicken and mushroom curry 58

Mowgli coleslaw chicken bowl 57

mushrooms

curry house prawn and mushroom omelette 102

Korean noodles 166

monsoon chicken and mushroom curry 58

mussels: ginger and garlic mussels with lime leaves 101

N

noodles

Aunty Geeta's string pudding 179

Korean noodles 166

minced pork and glass noodle broth 90

nuts

Aunty Geeta's string pudding 179

cauliflower, sugar snap and almond curry 122

chicken, coconut and pineapple curry 39

chicken korma 45

courgette and cashew curry 118

courgette and spiced peanut salad 152

mango chicken curry 36

Rice Krispie bhel puri 138

O

omelette: curry house prawn and mushroom 102

onions 18

ginger beer, onion and broccoli bhajis 141

last-minute lamb burgers 74

Mowgli coleslaw chicken bowl 57

pink pickled 74

Rice Krispie bhel puri 138

P

paneer: date-spiced 144

papaya: chicken papaya and green bean keema 60

paprika chicken 40

parsnip: little sparrow pea soup 53

pasta

godfather pasta 165

lemon chicken pasta 162

197

oozy tuna and apple pasta bake
168

six-minute tomato pasta 160

peanuts

courgette and spiced peanut salad
152

Rice Krispie bhel puri 138

pears: wild garlic and lamb salad 89

peas

keema toasties 72

little sparrow pea soup 53

peppers

after-school pepper pot 84

Korean noodles 166

pine nuts: spiced lamb and apricot
wraps 68

pineapple: chicken, coconut and
pineapple curry 39

pork

ginger beer pork 78

minced pork and glass noodle broth
90

potatoes

beetroot and back-of-the-fridge curry
128

cauliflower, sugar snap and almond
curry 122

crunchy poppy seed potatoes 134

wild garlic and lamb salad 89

prawns

curry house prawn and mushroom
omelette 102

prawn and broccoli curry 104

puddings

Aunty Geeta's string pudding 179

coconut and chia seed pots 182

R

raita: gherkin and coriander 107

rice

after-school pepper pot 84

black cardamom rice 27

Rice Krispie bhel puri 138

S

salads

courgette and spiced peanut salad 152

melon and feta salad 148

salmon

gin and tonic salmon 98

mango and coriander salmon 110

tamarind salmon curry 108

sandwiches

Indian fish finger sandwich 107

keema toasties 72

sausages: godfather pasta 165

school-skive semolina cake 174

seafood

curry house prawn and mushroom
omelette 102

ginger and garlic mussels with lime
leaves 101

semolina: school-skive semolina cake 174

shallots: aubergine and shallot curry 130

shortcuts 20–2

soups

little sparrow pea soup 53

minced pork and glass noodle broth 90

super-simple tomato and nigella soup
121

spices 15–17

spinach 22

chicken and spinach curry 42

chicken dhansak 34

crunchy poppy seed potatoes 134

keema toasties 72

spinach and chickpea curry 124

spinach meatball curry 80

steak: rare spice-rubbed steak 71

store cupboard 24–5

street-hawker sweetcorn 147

string pudding, Aunty Geeta's 179

sugar snaps: cauliflower, sugar snap and almond curry 122

sumac lamb steaks 83

sweetcorn: street-hawker 147

T

tandoori

quick angry chicken 46

tandoori lamb chops 77

tea: traditional masala chai 188

tomato ketchup: sticky chicken thighs 51

tomatoes

after-school pepper pot 84

chicken and spinach curry 42

chicken dhansak 34

chicken papaya and green bean keema 60

courgette and spiced peanut salad 152

eggs and watercress curry 155

godfather pasta 165

green bean and mango dahl 133

keema toasties 72

little sparrow pea soup 53

million-dollar dahl 116

monsoon chicken and mushroom curry 58

oozy tuna and apple pasta bake 168

paprika chicken 40

prawn and broccoli curry 104

six-minute tomato pasta 160

spiced butter bean curry 127

spiced lamb and apricot wraps 68

spinach and chickpea curry 124

spinach meatball curry 80

super-simple tomato and nigella soup 121

tamarind salmon curry 108

tuna: oozy tuna and apple pasta bake 168

turkey: yoghurt and coriander turkey with tenderstem broccoli 54

W

watercress: eggs and watercress curry 155

watermelon: melon and feta salad 148

wild garlic and lamb salad 89

wraps: spiced lamb and apricot 68

Y

yoghurt

Bengali fish curry 96

gherkin and coriander raita 107

mango and mint fool 180

mango and mint lassi 186

quick angry tandoori 46

school-skive semolina cake 174

tandoori lamb chops 77

ten-minute, late-night kebabs 86

yoghurt and coriander turkey with tenderstem broccoli 54

199

INDEX

Acknowledgements

A huge thank you to everyone who was involved in the making of this book. On the editorial side I would like to thank my publisher, Fiona Robertson, and Dan Hurst, my project and copy editor. Also, thanks to the larger editorial team, Brittany Willis and Ella Chappell, for checking everything so diligently.

For the photography team, thank you to Yuki Sugiura for the wonderful food photographs and to my friend Peter Goodbody for the pictures of me and my family. Thank you also to Claire Bassano, for her food styling and humour, along with Andy Mountfield – they were both such merry recipe testers.

Thanks also to Rachel Vere for sourcing beautiful props and art directing the shoot, and to Glen Wilkins, Karen Smith and Kieryn Tyler for their wonderful design work on the book. Also, to Uzma Taj, who oversaw the production aspects of the book. In sales and marketing, I would like to thank Laura Whitaker-Jones, Isabelle Panay, Rachel Gladman and Fiona Smith.

Finally, my family are who I live for, cook for, sweat for and fear for … but it is through my husband Zoltan, who helps keep the home fires stoked, that many of my fears are burnt away.

Nisha Katona

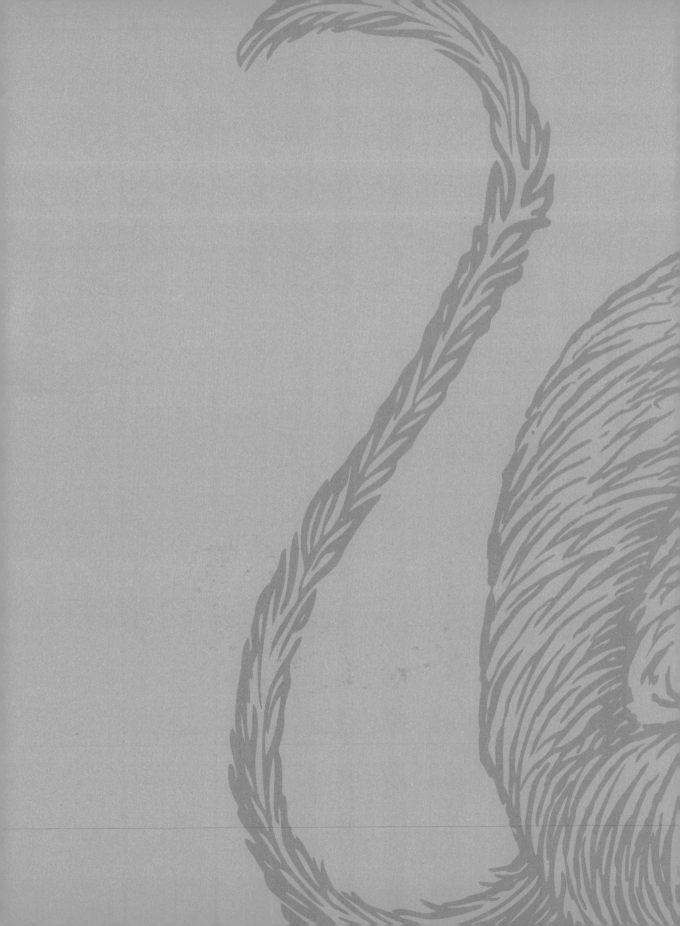